THE Brain-Compatible Classroom

USING WHAT WE

KNOW ABOUT LEARNING

TO IMPROVE TEACHING

Laura Erlauer

ASSOCIATION FOR SUPERVISION AND CURRICULUM DEVELOPMENT
ALEXANDRIA, VIRGINIA USA

Association for Supervision and Curriculum Development
1703 N. Beauregard St. • Alexandria, VA 22311-1714 USA
Telephone: 800-933-2723 or 703-578-9600 • Fax: 703-575-5400
Web site: http://www.ascd.org • E-mail: member@ascd.org

ASCD publications present a variety of viewpoints. The views expressed or implied in this book should not be interpreted as official positions of the Association.

Printed in the United States of America.

s02/2003

ISBN: 0-87120-748-6   ASCD product no.: 101269

Library of Congress Cataloging-in-Publication Data

Erlauer, Laura, 1966–
    The brain-compatible classroom : using what we know about learning to improve teaching / Laura Erlauer.
        p. cm.
Includes bibliographical references (p.   ) and index.
    ISBN 0-87120-748-6 (alk. paper)
    1. Learning.   2. Teaching.   I. Title.

LB1060 .E75 2003
371.102—dc21   2002153713

12 11 10 09 08 07 06 05   12 11 10 9 8 7 6 5 4 3

DEDICATION

I dedicate this book to my children . . .

three by birth
and
five hundred each year by employment

The Brain-Compatible Classroom
Using What We Know About Learning to Improve Teaching

Preface and Acknowledgments

THIS BOOK IS NOT WRITTEN BY A DOCTOR OF NEUROLOGY, OR A SCIENTIST, OR A researcher, but rather by a teacher (turned principal) who loves children and learning. I attended a seminar by Robert Sylwester in the early 1990s where he talked a lot about how the brain functions. As I sat in the audience, I came to the realization that I was a teacher who knew very little about how the brain actually learns. I was sparked and motivated, deciding I ought to be a "learning expert" before I could claim to be doing an expert job of teaching.

Over the next few years, I attended numerous conferences and read hordes of books and articles dealing with brain-based learning. As I implemented my new knowledge and strategies in my classroom, I saw students enjoying school, being challenged, engaging in their work, and achieving at higher levels than before. My enthusiasm bubbled over as I shared some ideas with colleagues. I spoke at some local and national conferences and other school districts, sharing practical ways to use brain-based learning theory in classrooms. Following the 2000 Annual ASCD Conference in New Orleans, I received a phone call from Joyce McLeod, an acquisitions editor for ASCD, who said she had been in my audience and wondered what I thought about writing a book. I have enjoyed developing this book with her.

Although writing a book has been an exciting challenge, I get (and probably give) a more enthusiastic charge from speaking to people about brain-compatible learning than writing about it. I want the excitement about learning to be contagious. It is more difficult for me to spread excitement through the written word than if we could be chatting person to person. So as you read this book, try to picture a person bubbling with enthusiasm about the topic, laughing and joking about children, handing you a Koosh Ball and talking about dendrites, and walking around, gesturing with my hands because I'm too charged up to stand behind a podium. I have tried to write this book in a nontechnical, conversational tone to make it an easy and enjoyable read. I did not want it to be a textbook. Textbooks can be boring, and boring is not good for the brain. Each chapter gives a simple summary of many other wise people's research on the brain and how it learns, and then gives real-life examples and anecdotes for you to use or modify for your own students.

I would like to thank all the teachers whose terrific ideas and strategies I share with you in each chapter. I admire their knowledge and skills and feel glad for their fortunate students. I thank my three wonderful children, Chad, Brent, and Lisa, who were patient when sometimes it seemed as though mom's computer must be her best friend. I thank Joyce McLeod and Deborah Siegel, who fixed all my goofy writing errors and gave me just the perfect editing recommendations. I thank my parents for being my best teachers—they knew what kids' brains needed before the current brain research came out. And I thank Gary, who invited me to that first seminar that improved my whole career and who, so many years and circumstances later, has invited me to marry him, improving my whole life.

Introduction

THE FIELD OF EDUCATION HAS ENTERED AN EXCITING AND CRUCIALLY IMPORTANT era—the brain era. We now know a great deal about the human brain and the biology of learning, and new discoveries are continually adding to that knowledge. One exciting facet of this knowledge explosion is the fact that people in general, not just neuroscientists, physicians, and psychologists, are interested in the findings and implications. Mass media and the popular press are highlighting brain-related topics that affect typical people. Average citizens, and parents in particular, are proving to be avid consumers of this information.

Until recently, our knowledge about the human brain was limited to what we could learn through the study of injured brains during surgery or from autopsies. Advances in medical technology over the past two decades—positive emission tomography (PET) scans and functional magnetic resonance imaging (MRI)—allow physicians and scientists to actually see how the brain functions while it is thinking or performing tasks. The implications of the current research on living brains are staggering, not only for the medical field, but also for the field of education. Educators are becoming privy to the biology of learning and therefore can discover which teaching practices actually maximize learning.

While many teaching methods have worked for decades, educators have found that some strategies haven't worked well at all. Tradition, intuition, and trial and error have been the basis for much of the instruction used in our classrooms. Today, education is poised to move beyond tradition for tradition's sake. Although we certainly have not uncovered all there is to know about the brain and learning, the medical field has given us some concrete, physiological data to consider when developing and implementing teaching strategies. Most undergraduate training of teachers has been based on how the adult should act, or how the teacher should teach. It is now time to study how the children act, how the learners learn. Educators can and must become learning experts. It is time to discover, from a physiological perspective, why particular teaching strategies have always worked and what new teaching and learning methods will be even more successful. Educators working in brain-compatible environments can develop an unprecedented professional competence that will enable students to reap the rewards of powerful, successful learning.

The Process of Change Toward Brain-Compatible Learning

If you're not riding the wave of change, you may end up under it! Isn't that what the inspirational greeting cards and calendars say about change? As we learn more about the brain, teachers will be expected to gain a thorough understanding of the learning process and, consequently, improve teaching practices in accordance with how the brain learns best. Making the change to a brain-compatible learning environment in a classroom does not happen overnight, and educators will probably never be able to say that they have completed their learning about brain-based instruction and how to apply it in their classrooms. We may never discover all there is to know about how the human brain works.

The good news for educators is that although it will take a lot of time and effort to develop a brain-compatible classroom, no teacher is starting from scratch. Every teacher out there is already successfully implementing effective teaching practices. Many traditional instructional strategies are, and have always been, brain compatible. Some of the ideas and brain-based practices may be radically different from what is seen in traditional classrooms, while others may involve slight modifications from typical procedures. Brain-based education is not a process by which a teacher disposes of all traditional practices and starts over. Rather, educators can learn, share, try, reflect, modify, and institutionalize new teaching methods and classroom practices slowly and deliberately.

Hard work and lots of time are always a part of an effective change process. If change seems too easy, it probably is not a true, enduring change. Some professionals and some of the literature on school change assume that adoption is the same as implementation. Adoption of an innovation is simple. It is the implementation that takes the time and effort. Even successful implementation of a change in a school setting is not enough. If lasting improvement is to occur, the new practices must be sustained over a long period of time in order to become part of "the way we do things here."

Prior to learning more about brain-compatible instructional strategies, it is useful to have some background information regarding how an individual will naturally progress through stages of change when applying these strategies or practices. The Concern-Based Adoption Model, shown in Figure I.1 (Hord, Rutherford, Huling-Austin, & Hall, 1987) describes the changing feelings of people as they learn about a proposed change, prepare to use it, use it, and modify it as a result.

Everyone involved in organizational change must understand that individuals go through these stages at different time periods and for varying lengths of time. Don't feel frustrated and give up too early. You may have to work through difficulties before operations can proceed smoothly. As Michael Fullan (1993) articulates, "Clarity must be achieved at the receiving end more than at the delivering end."

FIGURE I.I
Stages of Concern Related to Change

Degree of Concern	Stages of Concern	Expressions of Concern by Staff
0	Awareness	"I am not concerned about brain-based learning."
1	Informational	"I would like to know more about brain-based learning."
2	Personal	"How will brain-based learning affect me?"
3	Management	"I seem to be spending all my time getting brain-based materials ready."
4	Consequence	"How is my use of brain-based strategies affecting kids?" or "How can I refine the strategies to have more impact?"
5	Collaboration	"How can I relate what I am doing to what others are doing?"
6	Refocusing	"I have some ideas about something that would work even better."

Adapted from *Taking Charge of Change*, by S. M. Hord, W. L. Rutherford, L. Huling-Austin, and G. E. Hall, 1987, Alexandria, VA: ASCD.

Overview of the Seven Brain-Compatible Fundamentals

Many authors, including Caine and Caine, Jensen, Sylwester, Wolfe, McGeehan, Gardner, Goleman, Kovalik, and Sousa, have taken some of the latest scientific medical findings related to the brain and applied them to learning. In addition, many quality resources are available to anyone who wants to learn about detailed topics concerning brain-based learning. Books and articles give information about the physical sections of the brain and their functions, music and the brain, multiple intelligences and learning styles, the best foods for the brain, emotional intelligence, physical movement and the brain, classroom environment and teaching implications tied to the brain, and so on. Chapter 1 gives teachers a quick and basic overview of the parts of the brain and their functions. Chapters 2 through 9 compile, organize, and review the conclusions of the experts in terms of generalities or fundamentals that every teacher should know. Within each chapter are specific teaching strategies to use immediately as well as teachers' examples of classroom applications of brain-compatible instructional strategies. The following is a brief summary of seven brain-compatible fundamentals:

Seven Brain-Compatible Fundamentals

Emotional Wellness and Safe Environment

How are students' emotions linked to memory and learning? How do stress and emotions affect students' learning?

Teachers can establish a classroom and school environment that is fun and safe, and, therefore, more brain-compatible for learning.

The Body, Movement, and the Brain

Why do oxygen, water, sleep, certain foods, and movement affect students' brains and their learning?

Teachers can make adaptations to their physical classrooms and teaching techniques and educate parents about health-related issues to help children learn.

Relevant Content and Student Choices

Why does the brain remember some information and skills more readily than others? How, when, and why should we offer students choices?

Teachers can engage emotions and link new information to prior knowledge to make learning more meaningful for students. They can also increase motivation and memory, and accommodate ability levels and learning styles by offering choices to students. Information, practical strategies, and classroom examples are provided on project-based learning, multiple intelligences, learning styles, differentiated assessments, and involving students in decision making.

Time, Time, and More Time

What three time elements dramatically affect when and how well students learn?

Teachers can use the three time elements (time on task, time for comprehension, and opportune learning time periods in a child's life) in the classroom to increase learning.

Enrichment for the Brain

Is enrichment just for gifted kids?

Teachers can heighten learning for all students through the use of many enrichment practices, from using music in lessons to some bulletin board displays.

Assessment and Feedback

What forms of assessment are and are not brain compatible?

Teachers can use forms of assessments that enhance the learning process. Feedback should be prompt, specific, from a variety of origins, and built into the learning process.

Collaboration

How and why do students learn effectively through collaborating with others, both adults and peers?

To optimize learning in the classroom, teachers can apply the fact that the human brain is a social brain.

As scientists discover more about how the brain learns, educators are freed from the pendulum swing of instructional practices that come and go. Through the knowledge and understanding of the research about how human brains learn, educators can make informed decisions about what constitutes best practices in our schools and for our children. Brain-based learning is not a trend. The term "brain-based" may have been the new, catchy phrase four or five years ago. The term may even be fading in popularity as you read this. However, that does not mean teaching in accordance with how the brain learns is going out of style. As we learn even more about the brain's learning abilities and functions, educators will continue to improve their teaching methods to correspond with new findings. In fact, if or when the use of the expression "brain-based" or "brain-compatible" does decrease, it should be considered a sign of success. It may mean that teaching with the brain in mind has been institutionalized. We won't need to use a catchy phrase to show that we are applying the biology of learning in just some locations or instances because we will be applying it in our teaching and learning all the time. Brain-compatible learning has a medical, physiological basis, and this knowledge actually helps educators move away from trendy but ineffective innovations in the field.

1

A Walk Through the Brain

BECAUSE THIS BOOK'S MAIN FOCUS IS ON THE DAY-TO-DAY CLASSROOM APPLICATIONS of brain-based research, I will not attempt to provide you with a thorough description of the physical brain and all its functions. However, it is beneficial for teachers to have at least a general awareness of how the brain physically functions. This knowledge can help teachers understand their students' needs or reactions and may provide a physiological basis for certain instructional decisions. So, let's take a quick walk through the brain.

Imagine yourself in a time and place where plants cover the land, fish fill the sea, and reptiles are the only creatures you encounter. There are no computers, light bulbs, or even arrowheads. You do, however, see a lizard. Not a particularly cute critter and certainly not very intelligent. The lizard has a primitive brain that instinctually helps the animal survive. This animal's life revolves around vital functions: blood pumping, breathing, eating, reproducing, and so on.

A part of the human brain is lizard-like—the *reptilian* portion of our brains. Put on your galoshes and wetsuits because we're walking into the brain. The brain weighs only about three pounds and consists of lots of water, so it may get messy in here (Jensen, 1997). Our reptilian brain, or brain stem, is located at the base of the brain and is connected to the spinal cord (see Figure 1.1). The brain stem produces many of the brain's chemical messengers and controls the automatic, vital functions of the body that ensure our survival; it adjusts and maintains the body's heart rate, blood pressure, and breathing. The brain stem receives messages through the spinal cord from the five senses and reacts through the reticular activating system (RAS). This system filters out stimuli that are unimportant

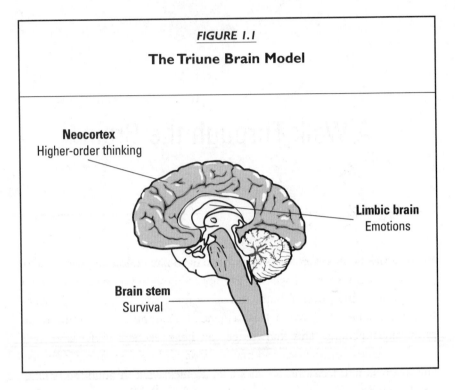

FIGURE 1.1

The Triune Brain Model

and sends the important messages to other parts of the brain or body for physical reaction or for conscious consideration (Wolfe, 2001). The RAS may make us unaware of the everyday aroma of our households; we are used to the smell of our own homes. However, when we walk into someone else's home, we may notice it has a distinct aroma. When you smell smoke, the RAS may even raise your heart rate and send a message to the conscious part of your brain, allowing you to think about fire and check your own safety status.

A related personal experience I have had with my sense of smell is directly correlated to my reptilian brain. During each of my three pregnancies, my sense of smell was dramatically heightened. For example, prior to being pregnant I played bingo and could not detect any odor emanating from the ink dabber unless I held it right under my nose. When I played bingo again when I was pregnant, not only could I smell the same dabber's odor from an arm's length, but the smell was so strong that it literally burned my nose. When I asked a neurologist at a seminar about this phenomenon, she explained it was my reptilian brain kicking in, protecting my unborn child from harm. Presumably a bingo dabber is of no threat. However, just as a mother lion's sense of smell is crucially important in detecting predators nearing her cubs, my brain's RAS was instinctually helping to protect me while in a more vulnerable state of pregnancy. Although I wasn't in danger of a predator attacking, the reptilian portion of the brain is essentially the same as it was back in the days of just lizards roaming the land. I was pregnant, so the reptilian portion of my brain heightened my sense of smell as an automatic protection function.

The next part of our journey continues to take us through the unconsciously functioning portions of the brain. The cerebellum, located behind the brain stem just above the very top of your neck, controls basic muscle movements and motor skills. The human cerebellum, like the brain stem, is not much different from the corresponding part of an animal's brain; it helps us walk or grasp or automatically remember how to perform other motor skills that we really don't need to think about. As we travel further up in the brain from the brain stem and cerebellum, we move beyond the lower, reptilian brain into the next level of evolutionary brain development—the limbic brain, which is the location of the *limbic system* (Howard, 2000). The limbic brain deals with eating, drinking, sleeping, hormones, and the emotions (Sprenger, 1999).

The final area of the brain is the forebrain, which contains the thalamus, the hypothalamus, the amygdala, and the neocortex, among other structures (see Figure 1.2). The thalamus helps control the body's vital functions and transfers some sensory information up to the cortex (the thinking part of the brain). The hypothalamus, located right below the thalamus, plays a role in regulating our bodies' normal physical functioning like temperature, sleep, hunger, sex drive, and fight-or-flight response to danger. The amygdala and hippocampus are also responsible for fight-or-flight responses. The amygdala works with the thalamus to decide what stimuli are dangerous and should be sent to the thinking part of the brain for processing. The hippocampus is one of the memory portions of the brain. It controls your immediate memories and decides what to do with them, including whether they should be acted on or sent to long-term memory (Wolfe, 2001).

The last part of our walk through the brain takes us into the largest portion, called the upper brain or the *neocortex.* The cortex is the portion of our brains that strongly distinguishes us from animals. It is the part of the brain responsible for high-level thinking, problem solving, language, planning, vision, pattern recognition, and so on. It differs from the lower

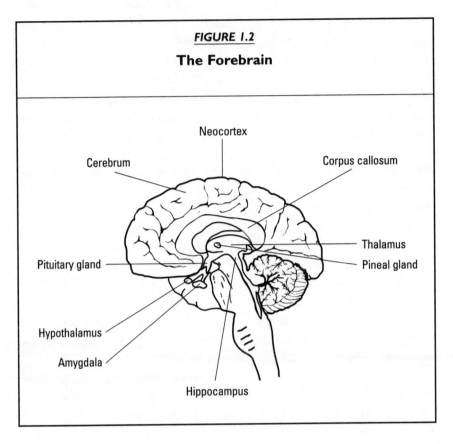

FIGURE 1.2

The Forebrain

brain in that some of the neocortex's functioning is on a conscious level. When thinking through a problem, we know our brains are working. When we are reading a book or listening to someone, we are aware of the task at hand and are consciously putting effort toward our behaviors or actions (Jensen, 1997). The cortex consists of four main lobes with different functions (Wolfe, 2001).

• **Frontal lobes.** These lobes are located in the front of the brain and stretch up and back from the forehead. These lobes are responsible for all high-level, conscious thinking, such as contemplating choices and making decisions. The frontal lobes also control sensorimotor planning, such as positioning and moving fingers to thread a needle. This part of the brain has continued to develop and expand through evolution more than any other part of the human brain.

• **Occipital lobes.** These lobes are located in the back of the head and are responsible for processing visual information. They process information about objects, colors, motion, and distance, and connect this information with past experience and memories to provide meaning.

• **Temporal lobes.** These lobes are located above the ears and are responsible for processing auditory information. They distinguish differences in sound, pitch, and loudness and determine their significance.

• **Parietal lobes.** These lobes are located in the top, back portion of the brain and are responsible for spatial awareness and for processing and analyzing sensory stimuli. They also play a role in maintaining focus or attention.

At the meeting point of the occipital, temporal, and parietal lobes are Broca's Area and Wernicke's Area. These areas are responsible for producing and comprehending speech.

As we have journeyed through the brain, you may have noticed the 100 billion or so brain cells (neurons) we walked by on our route. These billions of neurons alone do not make the brain intelligent. It is when the neuron's dendrites (long tentacles that look like tree branches) reach out and connect to another neuron's dendrites that learning occurs. These connections, or synapses, are the pathways for new learning. When an infant is born, he or she may have trillions of brain cells. However, only the neurons that form connections to other brain cells survive (Jensen, 1998). Adults have fewer brain cells than newborn babies, but all of the adults' neurons are connected with dense branches of dendrites (Howard, 2000).

We have come to the end of our walk through the brain. Take off your wetsuit and galoshes and step back into your classroom now. Considering the physical and functional attributes of the brain, what are the implications for your classroom and students? Consider the fact that every brain, due to its different dendrite connections, experiences, and memories, is as different as each individual's fingerprints. This means that every student you will ever have in a class has different backgrounds, needs, abilities, and wants, and it's your job to see to it that all these different brains learn. Whew! And you thought you were tired from our journey through the brain. The thought of reaching all those unique brains is exhausting. Thankfully, they almost all have some similarities in how they learn best. Chapters 2 through 8 will provide samples and strategies of brain-compatible learning that you can immediately implement in your classroom to help your students grow billions of dendrite connections in their brains.

2

Emotional Wellness
and a Safe Environment

TAKE A MOMENT TO RECALL YOUR MOST MEMORABLE SCHOOL EXPERIENCE. TYPI-cally when a group of adults is asked to do this half the crowd will tell a funny story while the other half will recount a negative, humiliating, or fearful experience. Whether positive or negative, all the memorable experiences shared will be filled with emotions. Our most powerful memories are laden with emotions. As you thought of your own school experience, those original emotions were perhaps rekindled, triggering a smile or frown on your face.

Because memories are so closely tied to emotions, teachers bear a heavy responsibility; every day they evoke emotions and mold memories in each of their students. The limbic area of the brain contains the amygdala, hippocampus, and thalamus/hypothalamus. These structures are involved, at least partially, with emotions, memory, and control of physical responses to stress, respectively (Howard, 2000; Jensen, 2000). Long-term memory is permanent learning and is a process affected by physical and emotional components.

When new information enters the brain through any of the five senses, the thalamus and hypothalamus quickly determine whether the information needs immediate attention or even fight-or-flight action or whether more "normal" brain processing is appropriate. The thalamus then disperses the new information to the amygdala and to the cortex. The amygdala decides the amount of emotional relevance attached to the information, while the cortex, the thinking part of the brain, begins the process of sorting the information, making sense of it, and categorizing it for long-term memory. The whole process of sorting stimuli and sending them into short-term or working memory usually occurs in less than 20 seconds (Wolfe, 2001).

The working memory can hold a small amount of information just long enough to determine if it is knowledge that is important or worthy of being remembered for a longer period of time. The hippocampus is the part of the brain responsible for memories of the immediate past and for eventually sending information to the cortex for long-term storage. The memory functions in the hippocampus are affected by the hormones and proteins released due to emotional responses. As the new information in the working memory begins to be recognized by the brain, new synapses occur or old ones are strengthened. A synapse is the process whereby dendrites from one neuron, or brain cell, attach to another neuron, making connections that cause learning to occur. Any emotional arousal, positive or negative, will spark the production of particular hormones and proteins. These proteins settle around the synapse, strengthening the connection (Howard, 2000). For students, this means emotionally important content learned in school is very likely to be permanently remembered.

The close tie between emotions and memory can be a double-edged sword for educators. As we've learned, permanent learning almost always has an emotional component. Teachers can use this knowledge productively by fostering positive emotions in their students while learning, thus strengthening the opportunity for remembering the academic concepts. Conversely, teachers who cause or allow stressful, threatening, or fearful occurrences in the classroom are building memories of those negative issues rather than important academic concepts. Because these students are under stress, their brains are operating in the limbic system rather than the higher-level neocortex, making learning much more difficult.

Emotional Intelligence

In addition to affecting our memory of concepts and events, emotions also drive our reactions and help us make decisions. Daniel Goleman, in his book *Emotional Intelligence* (1995), states that a person's emotional quotient (EQ) may be an even stronger predictor of happiness and success in life than his or her intelligence quotient (IQ). He describes a five-part model of emotional intelligence that was based on the studies of psychologist Peter Salovey of Harvard University:

- Self-awareness (monitoring one's own feelings).
- Self-management (managing the feelings so they do not disrupt life).
- Self-motivation (maintaining a positive, productive state).
- Other-awareness (detecting emotions in others and feeling empathetic).
- Relationship management (interacting smoothly with others using social skills).

We know, instinctually and now through brain research, that higher-level thinking and learning is more likely to occur in the brain of a student who is emotionally secure than in the brain of a student who is upset, stressed, or insecure. The first three components of Goleman's EQ model address these concepts. The last two components address the idea that the human brain can learn effectively through collaboration with others (Sousa, 1995).

In its entirety, the EQ model addresses people's abilities to monitor their own feelings, to be self-motivated, to recognize emotions in others and respond with empathy, and to act with social competence (Howard, 2000), all of which help to develop more satisfied people who are better prepared for learning and life.

Since the mid-1990s, educators and curriculum developers have been pushed to develop curricula to address these five major components of emotional intelligence. Some schools may address students' emotional intelligence through specific lessons, while others may weave it into everyday school experience. Regardless of the mode of delivery, these lessons help students understand their own emotions as well as those of others and foster an emotionally secure learning environment.

■ ■ ■

EXAMPLE: LESSON SPECIFICALLY ADDRESSING EMOTIONAL INTELLIGENCE
GRADE 2 GUIDANCE CLASS LESSON

Purpose: To help students develop relationship skills.

Background: Ms. Cole, a school guidance counselor, understands that the academics taught in other classes may not be important to a child if his or her emotional state is frail. For example, a student will not put his heart and soul into completing a solar system project and subsequently presenting it to the class if he has no friends and is hurt and embarrassed by ridicule he receives from his peers. To improve students' emotional intelligence, Ms. Cole teaches specific lessons twice a month, based on at least one of the five components of the emotional intelligence model.

Lesson: To help students develop and manage relationships with their friends, Ms. Cole holds a frank discussion with the students about making and keeping friends. The students brainstorm ways to make friends, define what constitutes a good friend, and identify ways to keep friends. She presents a video that shows examples of several ideas the class has discussed. She asks several students to take turns role-playing friendship skills, such as asking someone to play, dealing with a conflict, and politely declining an invitation from a friend.

EXAMPLE: INTEGRATING EMOTIONAL INTELLIGENCE INTO EVERYDAY SCHOOL PRACTICES
ELEMENTARY SCHOOL EXAMPLE

Purpose: To improve student behavior in individual classrooms and in the common areas of the school.

Reasoning: Immediate and logical consequences are usually the best way to deter students from repeating a negative behavior and the best way to induce students to repeat a positive behavior. Many classroom and school behavior-management programs rely heavily on consequences. An additionally helpful way to teach cause and effect, as well as the emotional intelligence elements of self-awareness, other-awareness, and self-management, is implementing the use of a "think sheet."

Procedures: A variety of these forms are used in many schools and should be tailored to what the staff at a school deems important for the student to reflect upon. At Jackson School our "think sheet" is found on the back of a referral slip. Referral slips are filled out by staff members and sent to the principal following a severe offense or as the result of a third offense of the same negative behavior, when other consequences have not improved the student's behavior. The "think sheet" is completed by the student with the help of the teacher, principal, or, ideally, a parent. Its purpose is to spur the child who has done something wrong to contemplate his or her behavior, how it affected others, the consequences involved, and, most productively, to think about how to improve.

■ ■ ■

The way students deal with their emotions has implications for their social and emotional wellness both in school and out of school, so teaching students how to understand and deal with their own emotions is an important topic for teachers to address.

Stress

Your body might tense up just reading the word. The physical reactions caused by stress originate in the brain. The stimulation causes the front part of the hypothalamus to work on calming the emotions, while the back part of the hypothalamus initiates the secretion of stress hormones, prompting physical reactions in the body. The occurrence, or anticipation, of a stressful situation causes changes in bodily processes (see Figure 2.1) as it gears up for fight or flight (Brynie, 1998).

A person facing a saber-toothed tiger ready to pounce will be thankful for these bodily changes. However, these physical reactions still occur in response to today's stressors. People do not need stronger muscles, keener vision, or faster-clotting blood to help with the stress they feel from job deadlines, financial strains, naughty children, divorce court, and speeding tickets. These same bodily processes that helped us survive long ago can cause actual risks to our health in today's world. Long-term stress can cause health problems, from relatively simple ailments such as headaches and skin rashes to chronic and dangerous disorders such as depression and heart disease.

FIGURE 2.1
Physiological Effects on Bodily Processes Due to Stress

Physiological Change	Effect on Bodily Processes
Increased metabolism of fat and glucose	Fuels body for quick action
Dilation of pupils	Provides keen visual perception
Constriction of heart arteries	Increases amounts of blood pumped to the heart and other muscles
Relaxation of bronchial tube	Allows for deeper breathing
Modification of blood chemistry	Makes clotting easier in case of wounds
Slowed digestion	Augments the blood supply to muscles

Sadly, children also have to deal with stress in their lives. Some children live in homes or attend schools where physical threats are prevalent. Even the relatively simple or typical stressors for children or young adults, such as friendship problems, home issues, being teased, feeling unworthy, homework deadlines, and peer pressure, can cause physical problems if the stress is prolonged over time.

Stress certainly affects students and their learning. As described in *Nature Neuroscience* (1998) Sonya Lupien, professor at Montreal's McGill University, found that high levels of cortisol produced by long-term stress caused shrinkage of the hippocampus, resulting in memory impairment. It is easy to understand how a student might have trouble memorizing multiplication facts if he or she is worried about a violent home life. If a student sits staring at the clock, dreading recess time because of daily teasing, the teacher cannot expect to have that child's full attention on a lesson.

Teachers can help students deal with stress in several ways. First, a teacher can help the student gain control of stressful situations. Stress usually stems from fear. By fostering a student's sense of confidence and power, the teacher builds up the student's control over many situations, thus reducing stress. Although educators cannot necessarily eliminate the stressors in their students' lives, they can help students limit some of those stressors and their effects. Simply having a teacher who cares enough to listen can help some students deal with stress. Teachers can refer students to a guidance counselor or psychologist for assistance. Students can be taught relaxation or coping skills to deal with the emotional and physical reactions they have to stressful situations. In cases of abuse, teachers should report their suspicions to the police, the social service department, or the school administrator, as mandated by district policy or local or state law. Another way a teacher can help students deal with stress is to establish a truly safe environment in his or her classroom and school. Classroom environment is discussed later in this chapter.

■ ■ ■

EXAMPLE: STRESS CAUSED BY POSTING SCORES IN CLASSROOMS
ALL GRADE LEVELS

Background: Terrence and Amanda are two 8th grade students who share the same teacher for language arts, social studies, and homeroom. Their teacher posts social studies unit test scores on a classroom wall, charts number of novels read each semester on a poster, and has students grade each other's weekly spelling tests and then read aloud the scores as she enters them in her grading book. Terrence is a straight *A* student. Amanda is a struggling student. They are both very stressed in this teacher's classes. Why?

Reasoning: Amanda is continuously embarrassed by her school performance and hates having the other 25 students know how poorly she is doing. Rather than working harder to do better to get to the top of the class, or even the middle, Amanda has essentially given up. Her attitude is "if you can't be the best, have fun being the worst." Her class clown behaviors kick in, and she enjoys the attention she receives laughing about her low grades, trying to prove it is funny to be at the very bottom of the bunch. Terrence, on the other hand, is under immense pressure to remain at the top of the class. He is a perfectionist who becomes a nervous wreck if another student happens to pass him up on one of the score charts. Remaining at the top doesn't make him feel much better though, because he is dubbed "the brain" and resented by many of his peers.

Issue: Some teachers believe that posting academic or behavioral achievement is motivating for a class. While it may motivate some, it is an ego-cruncher and a fear-builder for the majority of the students. Grades and other academic performance ratings are private and should be kept that way to help ensure a secure, safe environment in the classroom. Imagine sitting in a room of 25 peers and having some private information, such as your weight, being reported aloud. A bit unnerving, I would say. We don't need to put students through this unnecessary stress and infringement of privacy. In fact, in July 2000 the Tenth Circuit Court in *Falvo v. Owassa Independent School District* ruled that the Family Educational Rights and Privacy Act (FERPA) is violated by the practice of peer grading and having students call out the grades to teachers. Furthermore, posting a student's grade under his or her name or an identifying number, such as a social security number, also is in violation of FERPA unless a parent gives prior written consent (Bell, 2001). Although this court's decision was reversed by the U.S. Supreme Court during its 2001–2002 term, it does give educators something to carefully consider about their grading and posting practices (*Education Week,* 2002).

Preferred State: Even the most kind, respectful teacher may use a behavior or procedure that causes undue stress for students. Teachers cannot prevent all negative, stressful feelings for students but can anticipate stressors for students and work to avoid them as often as possible. Be cognizant of teacher behaviors that decrease and increase stress for students (see Figure 2.2).

■ ■ ■

Creating a Safe Environment

Students spend a large portion of their waking moments in schools. Therefore, they deserve to have safe and happy schools. Safety in schools has become a major issue in the United States in recent years. We may be

---

FIGURE 2.2
Teacher Behaviors That Affect Student Stress

To decrease stress for students	To increase stress for students
• Set clear classroom rules with predetermined consequences.	• Delegate punishments according to your mood at the time.
• Keep students' sensitive information, such as grades and personal issues, confidential.	• Post grades or assignment scores in the classroom for motivation; embarrass them into achieving.
• Speak respectfully to students, address them by name, get to know them as individuals, and make each person feel special.	• Point at students you wish to call on and always let them know who is boss by the tone of your voice.
• Use rubrics for assignments so students know the exact expectations for earning specific grades.	• Give pop quizzes to catch students who have not been studying.
• Smile, have fun teaching, and show a sense of humor.	• Yell at the students to keep them in line and never, ever smile.

entering an era where having metal detectors in school entryways becomes the norm, which may or may not be a bad thing. Debate does exist on whether there is actually more violence in schools than 10 years ago, or if there is simply more publicity now of the events that do occur. In either case, there may be a silver lining. School personnel seem to be learning and implementing more preventive safety measures in their buildings, including identifying and providing assistance to potentially violent, disturbed students. For the purposes of this book, however, I will be discussing emotional safety rather than physical safety.

When thinking about the environment of a classroom, the following quote exemplifies how influential a teacher can be:

> I've come to a frightening conclusion that I am the decisive element in the classroom. It's my personal approach that creates the climate. It's my daily mood that makes the weather. As a teacher, I possess a tremendous power to make a child's life miserable or joyous. I can be a tool of torture or an instrument of situations, it is my response that decides whether a crisis will be escalated or de-escalated and a child humanized or de-humanized (Ginott, 1975).

Self-esteem and emotional wellness are necessary to reach one's potential as a student and as a person in general. It is the teacher who develops a safe, happy classroom environment to nurture those two traits. To cultivate and maintain such an environment is an individual, personal process for each teacher. What works well for one teacher may not work well or feel appropriate for another. But somehow or some way, every teacher needs to establish an emotionally secure classroom setting because brain research tells us that is the best climate for learning. The following general categories should be attended to in some fashion in order to develop a comfortable learning environment:

- Sense of Community
- Expectations for Students
- Teacher Behaviors

The examples provided may or may not fit a particular teacher's style but are intended to foster thought and new implementation ideas.

Sense of Community

To help students feel good about themselves and secure in their environments, maintaining a sense of community is fundamentally important both in the individual classroom and in the school as a whole. The development of teamwork and mutual respect among students, among staff members, and between students and staff members results in a sense of community. This sense of community will foster acceptance, self-esteem, and collaboration, and will ultimately become a learning tool.

Sense of Community Within a Single Classroom

Students should be guided to understand that they may not all like each other or be best buddies, but they should treat each other with respect and kindness. A class should function as a family of sorts; classmates, like siblings, may not always agree or feel close, but when push comes to shove, they feel bonded and stand up for each other. Developing this rapport among peers does not happen overnight, nor does it take place without leadership from an adult. The teacher must teach social skills and model respectful behaviors consistently, even creating role-playing situations in the classroom to address potential situations and conflicts that may arise. The teacher needs to get to know the students individually and allow classmates to get to know each other individually as well. When students feel a part of a group, accepted for who they are, and connected to adults in the school, their self-esteem, effort, and participation is strengthened (Sergiovanni, 1992).

■ ■ ■

EXAMPLE: GROUPING STUDENTS FOR RAPPORT
AND TEAMWORK
ALL GRADE LEVELS

Purpose: To facilitate productive positive relationships and teamwork through grouping practices.

Reasoning: Arranging desks to seat groups of four to six students and then rotating the students in and out of those groups every few weeks helps to promote rapport and teamwork among the classmates. Students may end up sitting next to other people they don't like. That is okay; they need to work it out, just as in real-world situations. The teacher may need to guide these students through anger management or conflict resolution strategies. And, as in the real world, these students may have to end up separated from each other after all. Students may also end up sitting next to a best friend and chatting too much. That is okay too; they will have some natural consequences to cope with, just like in the real world. Listening to the teacher and following directions are typically classroom rules that these students are required to follow, just like everyone else in the class.

Procedures: Grouping students for lessons or project work can be done very deliberately by the teacher according to ability levels, learning styles, or peer relationships. Or groupings can be randomly assigned using a variety of methods. Both styles of groupings are very valuable, both for completing the academic task at hand and for learning how to relate to and cooperate with others.

Sample Strategy: Mrs. Rintelman, a 3rd grade teacher, uses a quick and easy way of randomly partnering up students for academic tasks. At the beginning of the school year, each student is given a sheet of paper displaying a clock with name lines next to each hour (12:00 with a line next to it, 1:00 with a line next to it, etc.). The kids walk around the room signing other's clocks. For example, if Katie signed Brian's 5:00 line, then Brian had to sign Katie's 5:00 line. Each student ends up with 12 names (designated partners) on his or her sheet.

During lessons, Mrs. Rintelman no longer has to tell her students to find a partner to work with, a practice that can take too much time and cause hurt feelings for the loners. Instead, Mrs. Rintelman simply tells the class to work with their 6:00 partner, for example. The students know to quickly check that clock-sheet to determine which classmate will be their partner, find that person in the room, and begin the work. If a teacher wants more partner assignment opportunities, the sheet can have two lines by each hour. The teacher can then tell the class to work with their 6:00 a.m. partners or 10:00 p.m. partners.

■ ■ ■

Sense of Community Within a Whole School

Beyond the four walls of a classroom, the students of the entire school also benefit from a sense of school community and teamwork. A school's colors, mascot, and school song help build a sense of camaraderie and pride in that community. A community service project completed by a school provides a common purpose where teamwork and pride are also fostered. Many schools promote collaboration through cross-grade-level projects or activities in which older students may help younger students. Here are a few ideas:

- Reading partners
- Help with zippers and boots during inclement weather
- Tutoring
- Tours of the school
- Hallway monitors
- Recess buddies

- Neighbor walkers, escorting to and from school
- Writing letters back and forth
- Guide for new students
- Art project helpers
- Bus seat buddies

Will a school ever be completely free from older kids teasing younger kids or stronger kids ridiculing weaker kids? Maybe not. However, if the school staff works hard to create an attitude of mutual respect and solidarity, students will feel a greater sense of community in a safe and happy environment.

■ ■ ■

EXAMPLE: COMMUNITY SERVICE PROJECT— HAT AND MITTEN TREES ELEMENTARY, MIDDLE, AND HIGH SCHOOLS

Purpose: To promote community service and responsibility in students.

Background: One of the most worthwhile yet simple community service projects I have seen is the collection of winter hats and mittens for less fortunate families. This program benefited both the needy recipients and the students gathering the hats and mittens, who felt satisfaction from helping others through a school-wide service program.

Procedures: In mid-November, each of the schools in the school district displays one or two imitation Christmas trees in the lobby areas. Notes are sent out to parents requesting that a new pair of mittens or a new hat be sent to school with one of their children. Most parents are very willing to purchase an extra one of these items as they do winter shopping for their own children. Before long, the trees are decorated with warm, colorful hats and mittens. One of the schools located near a senior citizen center/ nursing home established an additional side project with that center. The children made holiday cookies and homemade books to share with the residents, and some of the senior citizens donated hand-knit mittens and hats for the school's tree. On the last day before the winter vacation periods the hats and mittens were counted in order to inform the students how many needy children they helped by their generosity. All the donations were then taken to a local low-income assistance distribution center.

EXAMPLE: CROSS-GRADE-LEVEL PROJECT— LETTERS TO SANTA AND ANSWERS FROM ELVES *GRADE 7 AND KINDERGARTEN*

Purpose: To build cross-grade-level relationships that help children learn and also help foster positive self-esteem and social behaviors.

Reasoning: Ideas for cross-grade-level projects are as numerous as the benefits the students gain from the activities, from older and younger students reading books to each other to older and younger students working collaboratively to create a mural on a school wall. Cross-grade-level projects can even occur across several schools. However and wherever they occur, these working relationships can improve student academic achievement, social behaviors, and self-esteem.

Lesson: A kindergarten teacher and a 7th grade teacher from schools across town from each other implemented a writing project between the two grade levels. The kindergarten teacher had her students write letters to Santa. They worked hard on these letters using their immature knowledge of wording, sentence structure, and spelling. As you can imagine, the letters were filled with creative, naive questions and wishes for Santa expressed in their darling, inexperienced penmanship. The teacher often deciphered the letter on the back of the paper so it could be read. These letters were sent to "Santa's Workshop in the North Pole," which was actually a 7th grade classroom on the north end of town.

Each 7th grade student in the class received one of the letters to answer. Rather than having each student answer as if he or she were Santa, producing many different styles of handwriting, the teacher had each student pretend he or she was an elf writing on behalf of the busy Santa Claus. The students had a ball coming up with elflike names for themselves and writing responses to the letters. The assignment was tied to a lesson dealing with descriptive writing, and was graded accordingly. The vivid descriptions in the letters, detailing all that Santa and the elves were busy doing at the North Pole, were exciting for the kindergartners and their teacher. Even the local newspaper thought it was an original, delightful project and printed some of the kindergartners' letters and the 7th graders' responses for the townspeople to enjoy.

In classrooms where some students may be uncomfortable writing to Santa (for religious reasons) it might be best to try an alternative cross-grade project. Older students could write children's books for younger students to illustrate, or vice versa.

EXAMPLE: WHOLE SCHOOL CELEBRATION ASSEMBLIES
ELEMENTARY SCHOOL

Purpose: To foster positive school climate and pride in learning accomplishments.

Background: One of the most stimulating changes for me in moving from a teaching position to an elementary school principal position is the opportunity to frequently visit a wide variety of classrooms. These visits give me a global, schoolwide perspective of what each grade level is learning and the assortment of lessons, activities, and projects students complete in each unit. Other staff members and students, to a large extent, miss out on knowing about the exciting learning happening in different areas of the school. To remedy this, our school now has Celebration Assemblies at the end of each quarter of the school year. Celebration Assemblies are whole-school gatherings that have the feel of a pep rally. However, rather than celebrating a school sports team's success, we celebrate learning.

Procedures: The teachers bring their classes into the gymnasium as the song "Celebration" by Kool and the Gang blares through the room. When everyone is seated and the music ends, I enthusiastically welcome everyone and explain that we are meeting to celebrate their hard work. The students first learn the results (for the quarter) of our schoolwide behavior incentive program (which will be described in a later section in this chapter). We then celebrate reading as the librarian gives out numerous student awards for particular quantities of books read during the quarter. The last part of the assembly involves students and staff discovering what other grade levels have been learning.

Each grade level has about five minutes to share and celebrate their learning. This is done in a variety of ways. For instance, at one Celebration Assembly, a group of 3rd graders performed one of their trade books, *Why Mosquitoes Buzz in People's Ears,* with shadow puppets made with the art teacher's help. The kindergartners shared what they had learned in science by singing a song about the parts of a tree. A small group of 4th graders showed posters of the state's resources and explained their uses. Each quarter, each grade level shares some new learning in a unique, creative manner. The assembly ends with the students and staff leaving, some literally dancing out of the gym, to the "Celebration" song being played again.

Resulting Climate: The staff likes seeing what other classrooms have accomplished. Some of the older students enjoy seeing their younger siblings perform. And the younger students get very eager when they see this preview of "cool stuff" that they will learn in future grade levels. The sense of community sparked in these assemblies is obvious. The enthusiasm and pride for learning is fun, powerful, and invigorating.

■ ■ ■

Two tips for organizing your own Celebration Assembly or something similar:

- Keep it short. A celebration should never be boring—but it will be if the assembly runs longer than 45 minutes.
- Use uplifting music. This little "extra" adds big excitement to the event and becomes part of the ritual. I would recommend an uplifting song such as "Celebration" by Kool and the Gang, or "That's the Way (I Like It)" by KC and the Sunshine Band, or "Takin' Care of Business" by Bachman-Turner Overdrive, or "Gonna Fly Now/Theme from *Rocky*" by Bill Conti.

Expectations for Students

Clear academic and behavioral expectations for students are a part of a safe environment both in the classroom and in the entire school. Knowing what to expect minimizes the threat and stress of the unknown. Imagine suffering a serious consequence for doing something that you didn't know was wrong. Or imagine being held accountable for new knowledge that you didn't know you were supposed to learn. Both situations seem unfair and cause stress for students. The human brain seeks pattern and desires daily events to be logical and predictable (Jensen, 1998). Teachers can provide a safer learning environment by establishing clear expectations and logical consequences for students.

Academic Expectations for Students

Traditionally, coaches and teachers operate quite differently when working with groups of children. Coaches tend to teach for success. For example, suppose a coach is teaching the skill of dribbling a basketball. He or she first shows the children exactly what good, proper dribbling looks like. The demonstration may then be expanded by showing some exceptional, fancy-footwork-type dribbling that the kids may aspire to learn with extra effort. The coach shows common errors made when dribbling the basketball and clear-cut methods to correct bad dribbling habits. Coaches tend to continue modeling and giving pointers to the kids until the skill is learned.

The students are encouraged to help each other practice and learn the skill. Finally, when the dribbling is mastered, the coach displays pride in

28

the students with words of praise and high-fives, and they may all celebrate together with a group hug and cheer.

Teachers, on the other hand, traditionally teach curriculum in a different fashion. The skill, such as writing a descriptive paragraph, is explained once. The teacher may or may not ever actually model a good descriptive paragraph. The advanced student, who may know the skill already, writes an exceptional paragraph and receives a high grade. This student's work is not shown as a model. In fact, if this student does show his or her work to others or tries to help classmates, it might be considered cheating. Then later, after not much practice or guidance from the teacher, the student is tested to determine if the skill has been mastered. If the skill has not been mastered, typically there is no continued practice or refinement, just a low score in the teacher's grade book. If the skill has been mastered, there are no high-fives and fanfare, just a high score quietly recorded in the grade book.

Thankfully, recent teaching practices have changed from the pop-quiz mentality of trying to catch students not learning concepts to a coaching-type attitude of being upfront in telling students just what is expected and helping them reach that goal. Using rubrics is one way a teacher can ensure that students know the expectations of an assignment. A rubric clearly delineates what work earns what score by modeling or explaining requirements. When a student knows exactly what work earns an *A*, what work earns a *B*, and so on, ownership in the learning has been given to that student. Additional benefits of using rubrics include assessing students' work in an objective manner and communicating expectations and scoring of assignments to parents; it is easy to explain to a parent why his or her child earned that *D* when the work can be directly compared to the expectations and models provided on the rubric.

■ ■ ■

EXAMPLE: ASSIGNMENT RUBRIC
HIGH SCHOOL GRAPHIC COMMUNICATIONS CLASS

Graphic Communications Career Assignment
After researching a Graphic Communications career, write and type a two- to three-page report with findings of your research.

Also include a cover page with your report. Your typed report can have print no larger than 12 points, and must be double-spaced.

Objectives

At the conclusion of this lesson, you will be able to:
1. Identify a career in Graphic Communications that interests you.
2. Know what the job you chose entails.

Procedure

You are to pick out a job or career related to some form of Graphic Communications and complete the following research:

20 pts. **What:** State the job and define the responsibilities.

15 pts. **Education:** What type of schooling is required?

15 pts. **Where:** State where your type of job might be located—city, type of printing plant, size of plant, etc.

15 pts. **Outlook:** What is the outlook for this job? Is it growing? Is it new? Is it steady work?

10 pts. **Working Conditions:** Suit and tie everyday? Number of hours per day? Week? Work alone or with others?

10 pts. **Money:** What is the salary?

15 pts. **Sources of Information:** List where the information was obtained and provide a printed copy of Internet information.

15 pts. **Summary:** Why are you interested in this career?

10 pts. **Newspaper Ads:** Locate two different job openings in Graphic Communications. Cut them out and tape them onto a piece of paper to turn in.

16 pts. **Grammar:** Correct grammar, spelling, and sentence fluency.

10 pts. **Proofread:** Two other students must proofread your paper and initial afterward.

10 pts. **Length:** Must be two to three pages in length.

4 pts.   **Miscellaneous:** Miscellaneous bonus points for creativity, extra information, etc.

165 total possible points

Possible Graphic Communications careers to choose from: Layout Artist, Graphic Arts Research Scientist, Platemaker, Quality Control, Press Operator, Bindery Supervisor, Graphic Design, Photographer, Customer Service, Estimator, Web Press Supervisor, Web Roll Tender, Cutter.

■ ▦ ▦

Behavioral Expectations for Students Within Single Classrooms

Classroom rules need to be established and clearly explained at the beginning of the school year for all ages of students. While one teacher's rules may differ from the rules of the teacher in the room right next door, some continuity of rules within a school is beneficial. There may be a few rules that everyone in a school community believes are crucially important to the school's successful operation or climate. The staff should collectively decide on a common term or phrase to be used in each classroom for these one or two common rules. For example, a staff decides that there is no tolerance of violence in their school, and each classroom will have a rule addressing this behavior. Rather than having one teacher say "No hitting," while a different teacher says "Keep your hands to yourself," one common phrase, such as "Keep hands, feet, and other objects to yourself," should be used in each classroom. Using a common phrase eliminates confusion in the students' minds as to what is expected. Also, as they move up through the grade levels in that school, they will be held accountable for that same crucial rule by each teacher.

Many rules will and should vary from classroom to classroom due to differences in students' ages, expectations of each teacher, and particular procedures implemented in each classroom. Teachers usually find that students will be able to remember the rules best if there are no more than five of them. It is wise to keep the rules clearly posted in the classroom and to provide the parents and the principal a copy of the classrooms rules and the resulting positive and negative consequences for following or breaking those rules.

When establishing rules and consequences, it is useful to keep in mind that typically the goal is to have students be responsible for their own behaviors—this way they will learn the life skill of self-management. Therefore, students must understand the reasoning behind each rule and know the potential consequences if the rule is violated. The consequences should be logical and student-based—not labor intensive for the teacher. For example, if a parent is to be called about an infraction, make the child responsible for making that phone call and explaining his or her actions.

As a principal, it is very helpful to have each teacher's classroom discipline plan briefly but specifically outlined on one page. See sample in Figure 2.3.

I keep these in a readily accessible file so when a parent calls me to question a consequence his or her child has received I can explain, for example, that indeed the student is being kept in for three recesses because it is the established third-step consequence after the warning and conference with the teacher. The more important reason I require teachers to turn in a discipline plan is simply to ensure that each teacher *has* a carefully designed plan. Within acceptable parameters, it doesn't matter what terms individual teachers use for their behavior expectations (rules, guidelines, expectations, etc.) or specifically what they are, or the resulting consequences. It does matter that teachers consistently adhere to their plan because that is best for the students and most effective for classroom management. Regardless of what they are named, or how they are developed, clearly stated and enforced behavioral expectations give students a feeling of safety.

■ ■ ■

EXAMPLE: DEVELOPING CLASSROOM RULES
GRADE 5 AND GRADE 1 SAMPLES

Purpose: To establish classroom rules that are understood and followed by students.

Reasoning: The initial development of classroom rules is done in a variety of ways. Some teachers have found a few rules that work best for them and use those same rules year after year. Other teachers find it useful to have students participate in establishing

---

FIGURE 2.3

Classroom Management Plan

Teacher-Principal Classroom Management Worksheet

Teacher name: Debbie Pelky

Behavior rules/expectations for my classroom:
—Be a good listener.
—Raise your hand.
—Do your best work.
—Be kind to others.

Discipline plan for my classroom:

When a student breaks a rule:

1st time	verbal warning
2nd time	time out
3rd time	miss one recess
4th time	parents called
Severe clause	green discipline sheet (sent home for parent signature) sent to the principal

Other negative consequences that might be used:
Privileges taken away

Positive consequences/rewards used with my students:
Star award slips, stickers, achievement certificates, edible treats, hugs, prizes, free-choice time, praise.

Any students that require an individualized behavior plan and a brief summary of that plan:
Behavior modification charts to be sent home daily and signed by the parent. Possible use with _____ (ADD characteristics).

---

the rules so that they have more ownership of those guidelines. Either way, it is important that the students not only know the behavioral expectations but also why they are in place and what will happen when they are followed or not followed.

Sample 1: A 5th grade teacher, Mrs. Sloane, has her students help develop the rules through class discussion and debate. This ensures comprehension and ownership of the rules by the students. The class then writes up the rules as their class constitution, and each student signs the bottom of the page. This behavioral contract is permanently posted in the classroom.

Sample 2: Mr. Barnes, a 1st grade teacher, finds it most beneficial to use the term "choices" rather than "rules." He likes the students to understand that, just like in the real world, every action is a choice with logical consequences; they can make good choices and earn positive rewards, or make bad choices and earn negative penalties.

■ ■ ■

Behavior Expectations for Students Within a Whole School

Comparable to the discipline plan in an individual classroom, the schoolwide rules and consequences should be known by all members of the school community. Ideally, the staff members should have a hand in developing the rules and reviewing them to ensure they remain relevant and appropriate. The consequences for violating the rules, both negative and positive, should be logical and identified ahead of time whenever possible. Oftentimes, schoolwide behavior incentive programs operate competitively, pitting one student against another, one class against another, or one grade level against another. This does not establish a safe environment for students. Too often the result is that the "good" kids continue to behave well and earn the greatest number of rewards, while the "bad" kids give up trying to earn the rewards because they can never collect more than their peers.

■ ■ ■

EXAMPLE: BEHAVIOR EXPECTATIONS FOR STUDENTS IN THE WHOLE SCHOOL
AN ELEMENTARY SCHOOL'S BEHAVIOR INCENTIVE PROGRAM

Purpose: To promote favorable student behavior through a schoolwide program that fosters pride and teamwork.

Background: Jackson Elementary School implemented a new incentive program during the 2000–2001 school year with the following goal being developed by a representational group of staff members and then shared with students and parents:

Jaguar Superstar Incentive Program Goal: *To increase our students' favorable behaviors, manners, effort, and achievement through positive feedback during a schoolwide incentive program. Additionally, this program will build teamwork and an attitude of school spirit due to the fact it is a cumulative schoolwide goal, not a competition between classrooms or grade levels.*

Procedures: Individual students are awarded Superstar Awards (little slips of paper) for any desired behavior such as earning a high score, exhibiting strong effort, helping a friend, doing a favor for a teacher, lining up quietly after recess, and so on. The homeroom teacher saves his or her students' Superstar Awards for each quarter. Many teachers display them proudly in the classroom.

At the end of each quarter, each class counts how many Superstar Awards were earned and turns the number into the principal. Sometimes this counting is done in conjunction with a math lesson, such as making sets and counting by 10s. At the school's Celebration Assembly, I, as principal, reveal on an overhead projector six numbers. These are the quantities of awards earned in each of the six grade levels, kindergarten through 5th grades. I do not announce which grade earned which number. This removes any competition, keeping it purely a schoolwide goal to earn as many as possible. I add the numbers on the overhead projector to reveal the thousands of total awards earned in that quarter of the school year. A rocket ship is moved up a chart on the gym wall to show the year-to-date total. Our rocket ship is soaring toward a huge star with the year-end goal of 8,000 printed across it.

Reasoning: The important component of this incentive program is that the entire student body works toward the goal of earning 8,000 Superstar Awards during the course of the school year. There is no competition between students, classes, or grade levels to earn more than others; no teacher or grade level knows who earns how many awards. This promotes an incredible amount of teamwork among the students and a safe, fun environment in the school. It allows the students who do not typically earn many awards for good behavior or high grades an opportunity to put forth enough effort to perhaps earn only one award. However, just that one award can make the child feel good about his or her contribution toward the school goal without classmates knowing if he or she earned fewer or more than others.

Resulting Success: At the year-end Celebration Assembly, the students at Jackson School let out a deafening cheer when they learned they had earned 11,000 Superstar Awards! Because they reached the goal, I told the students they would receive three prizes. The first one was the feeling of pride, heard in their cheer, from setting a goal and working hard to achieve it. The second reward was an extra all-school recess for their superb teamwork. And the third was an individual reward (a star-covered bouncy ball) for their individual efforts throughout the school year. The students were excited when the next school year's goal was set for 10,000 Superstar Awards!

■ ■ ■

Teacher Behaviors

A common question asked teachers at a job interview is, "Is it important for your students to like you?" My answer used to be, "No. It is more important for my students to respect me, although I haven't had problems with my students not liking me." After rethinking the issue, my answer would now be an emphatic, "Yes, it is important!" It is true that a teacher must remain the adult in the relationship, not a buddy to the students. However, when students truly like the teacher, they enjoy being at school and are more dedicated to the class and learning. When you think back to your own favorite grade level or the class where you learned the most, did you like the teacher? I bet so.

A common factor shared by at-risk students who are not motivated to learn is the lack of a connection with an adult at school. The adult need not be a teacher, but simply someone who makes that student feel valued.

When a student does have good rapport and feels connected with his or her teacher, the potential is there for enthusiasm toward learning, interest and effort in the teacher's lessons, and on-task behaviors in the classroom.

■ ■ ■

EXAMPLE: POSITIVE ADULT BEHAVIORS MODELED FOR STUDENTS
ELEMENTARY SCHOOL LEVEL

Purpose: To establish and maintain a meaningful, positive rapport between teachers and students.

Background: As a teacher, I told my class at the beginning of the year that I had two favorite things in the world: children and learning, in that order. Then, I spent the rest of the year walking my talk. I showed the students how much I liked them just by doing little but oh-so-important things. I would genuinely listen when they talked to me. I was sure to learn each student's name by the end of the first day of school, and then address every child at least once every single day.

My goal was to make each student in the class feel like he or she was my very favorite student, even the one or two each year whom I found to be obnoxious. I would stand outside the classroom door with a smile on my face (even when I really didn't feel like smiling) and say things like, "Welcome to math." I shared bits of personal information about myself, such as my hobbies or brief stories about my own three children. I would remember something personal about each student to ask them about later, like, "How was the big soccer match last night?" I used humor in the classroom frequently, even if I turned out to be the only one giggling at my silly jokes—it still meant I was smiling. And, maybe most important, I showed excitement toward what we were studying—even if I had to fake it sometimes. Usually, regardless of the grade level I was teaching, I would learn something new through research with the students so I could genuinely model interest and enthusiasm for my students. Being the "guide on the side" rather than the "sage on the stage" is a much more enjoyable form of instruction for both teacher and students.

Now in my role as principal, I still tell my staff and students that my two favorite things in the world are students and learning. And I still walk the talk. I make sure I'm in classrooms every day showing enthusiasm toward learning. I build personal relationships with the students, learning as many of their 480 names as I can, chatting with them at lunch and recess times, delivering birthday cards to each student, and so on.

Survey Procedures: As a principal, I see which teachers are really liked by the students and which ones are not considered favorites. I thought it would be interesting to find out what characteristics the students identified in the most popular teachers. In an informal survey of 18–20 students, I asked students to identify their favorite teacher and tell me why they liked him or her.

Survey Results: The overwhelming answer was because "Mr. or Mrs. _____ is so nice."

When I probed to find out what made them "nice," three common answers emerged: he or she is fun; he or she doesn't yell; and he/she is funny. When I probed further, asking what was considered "fun," the answers revolved around making learning interesting, active, and enjoyable.

Teachers were not considered "nice" because they were overly lenient or gave away candy. In fact, the two or three teachers mentioned most often tend to be quite structured in their classroom management. They also tend not to have many discipline problems because their students are engaged in learning and don't have the time or the ambition to start problems in the classroom. I also believe their students are well behaved because they don't want to disappoint their favorite teacher and because the students care for him/her so much. Figure 2.4 defines some easy-to-implement teacher behaviors that promote a happy, caring classroom environment.

■ ■ ■

FIGURE 2.4

Specific Teacher Behaviors to Promote a Safe, Happy Environment

- Act respectfully toward students at all times.
- Learn students' names by the end of the first day of school.
- Personalize each student's desk or locker with a nametag.
- Smile a lot!
- Greet the students daily outside the classroom door.
- Share appropriate, amusing anecdotes about yourself.
- Remember personal information about each student and ask him or her about it.
- Use your sense of humor.
- Model the enjoyment of learning something new.
- Each week, invite a few students to share their lunchtime with you.
- Give each student a birthday card.
- Make learning interesting, active, and enjoyable.

Creating the Right Climate

The adults in the building—the principal, teachers, and other staff members—set the climate of the school and the classroom. Understanding how emotions can be used to strengthen learning helps a teacher effectively and purposefully link the two together during instruction. Furthermore, understanding how stress, low self-esteem, and negative emotions can inhibit learning also helps a teacher work with students.

A teacher's mood and behaviors, as well as the expectations of students and the sense of community established in the classroom, are crucial to the attitude and success of the students. One of my goals as a teacher was to make every student think he or she was my absolute favorite. Quite honestly, for some, I really had to put strenuous effort into faking it. Yet at the same time, I learned the phrase: "fake it 'til you make it." Sometimes it really worked in turning my inner feelings around about a student.

A safe, fun, nurturing environment is the best place for the human brain to develop and learn. Therefore, teachers' behaviors should reflect people who are respectful, caring, and enthusiastic about learning. When these behaviors are modeled, the result is students who are respectful, caring, and enthusiastic about learning.

Implementing Relevant Brain-Compatible Ideas:

Emotional Intelligence Tips
- Weave the five Emotional Intelligence model's components into everyday classroom life.
- Provide meaningful tasks for students to accomplish to foster self-esteem.
- Help students set reasonable goals to build a sense of pride.

Stress Tips
- Teach students stress management techniques such as time management, deep breathing, physical exercise, conflict resolution skills, and visualization.
- Establish classroom rituals and routines for students to count on, taking some of the stressful unknowns out of students' days.
- Search for help from appropriate officials when you suspect students are in threatening situations.

Sense of Community Tips
- Acknowledge individual and group efforts and special events through celebrations of some sort.
- Implement community service projects in which all students and staff participate.
- Foster team spirit through a school mascot, song, colors, etc.
- Develop programs for older students to work with younger students.

Expectations for Students Tips
- Have clear expectations for students both academically and behaviorally.
- Insist on respectful behaviors toward all people in the school.
- Enlist students' input in developing classroom rules.

Teacher Behavior Tips
- Show you care by making personal connections with students.
- Give frequent, positive feedback so students know how they are performing.
- Smile. Enjoy your terrific students. You have the best job in the world!

3

The Body, Movement, and the Brain

WHAT WE PUT IN OUR BODIES AND DO WITH OUR BODIES DIRECTLY AFFECTS THE brain and learning. Nutrition, sleep, and physical movement are crucial to the brain's survival, functioning, and learning. Poor nutrition, lack of sleep, and lack of physical activity affects the brain's ability to learn to its highest potential. In addition, if street drugs, misused prescription drugs, or alcohol are present in the body, the brain also does not learn to its highest potential.

Brain Foods

Eat your vegetables! Like most young children, you probably heard this command repeatedly from Mom at the dinner table. While those veggies may not put hair on your chest as Dad used to assert, it turns out that Mom had an intuitive glimpse into future brain research. That information now tells us that, indeed, fresh fruits and vegetables are very healthy for the brain. Also good for the brain are high-protein foods, such as fish, lean meats, and nuts (Jensen, 1998). Another tip you have probably heard over time is to eat several small meals each day rather than the traditional two or three big meals at established times. While a bias may be to treasure the big, established dinnertime for the value of conversation between family members, several small, healthy snacks during the day are good for the body and brain. Allowing students a quick healthy snack midmorning and even again midafternoon can give them a bit more energy to pay attention to lessons.

Aside from the benefits healthy foods provide the body, it has been found that some of these substances perform specialized functions in the brain. Calpain, for example, acts as a cleanser by dissolving protein buildup. This aids connections between dendrites. These connections, or synapses, form as new learning is taking place and link new information to prior knowledge. Cleaner dendrites and synapses means more efficient transmission and, therefore, better learning. Calpain is found in dairy products such as milk and yogurt, and in green vegetables (Jensen, 1998).

Brain chemistry is affected by different foods, and it may even make us crave certain foods. Eating proteins can increase the level of serotonin in the brain, which, in turn, is thought to influence brain and body functions such as sleeping, waking, paying attention—and even our moods. We may crave sweets for the sugar content that can increase alertness when eaten at certain times of the day. Or we may crave carbohydrates, such as breads or starches, which make our bodies feel more soothed or relaxed. Luckily for teachers, the brain's two favorite foods—oxygen and water—are quite abundant in schools.

Oxygen

The brain uses one-fifth of the body's oxygen although, at about three pounds, it may only weigh one-seventieth of the body's total weight. The highest-quality air contains more oxygen than carbon dioxide. Research tells us that breathing high-quality air increases both mental functioning and attentiveness, affirming that oxygen is good for the brain (Caine & Caine, 1994). In fact, many drugs that claim to improve memory and heighten attention simply increase the flow of oxygen to the brain. The use of air purifiers and filters is rapidly increasing. While these are often advertised as helping our lungs by pulling smoke or allergens out of homes, cars, and offices, they are also helping our brains.

Have you ever seen a lazy dolphin? You probably have not, because dolphins exchange about 80 percent of their body's oxygen with each breath, while humans exchange less than 20 percent (Jensen, 1998). Old, stale air is not energizing. Do you need to spend money on an air purifier to increase the oxygen to your students' brains? No. Open a window in your classroom whenever possible. Tell the kids to take a deep breath every now and then. Or, to have a little fun and increase the students' oxygen intake, give a big, broad yawn yourself and see how contagious it is.

Let students know that often people yawn not because they are tired, but because they need more oxygen for increased alertness.

Water

Water is the brain's second favorite food—right after oxygen. The old wives' tale that we need eight cups of water per day is absolutely correct—we need this water not just for the body, but also for the brain. The brain is made up of a higher percentage of water than any other organ in the human body. This means that dehydration can have a marked effect on the brain. Picturing a shriveled, dried-up little brain rolling around in a skull is a bit extreme, but picturing a lethargic student drooping in his or her desk is right on the money. This lethargy could be a result of dehydration and is not uncommon in schools (Sousa, 1995).

In addition to causing lethargy, a lack of water can also cause stress. When the percentage of water in the blood decreases, the salt level increases. Increased salt levels can cause muscles to constrict and blood pressure to increase, causing the feelings of tenseness and stress. Stress researchers found that within five minutes of drinking water, there is a marked decline in the hormones that elevate stress (Jensen, 1998). Does this mean you will be stress-free if you drink enough water? Should you carry a gallon of water and a straw around with you on the day your supervisor is observing in your classroom? Not exactly. Drinking a lot of water does not erase the factors causing the stress. However, some of the stress symptoms can be reduced when the body and brain are kept hydrated.

■ ■ ■

EXAMPLE: USE OF WATER BOTTLES IN SCHOOLS
ALL GRADE LEVELS

Purpose: To keep students hydrated during the school day.

Background: Students should be allowed more than the occasional drink at the water fountain at recess or as they pass between classes. Drinking water frequently during the day, as we have learned, can boost attention and lower symptoms of stress. Therefore, I propose allowing all students to have a bottle of water at their desks that may be refilled at recess times or times deemed appropriate by the teacher. I began allowing my students to have water bottles when I was teaching 3rd grade. Some of my colleagues would have a cup of coffee or a can of soda at their desks, which did not seem fair to the students, who were not allowed the same privilege.

Procedures: I began bringing bottled water to the classroom and allowed the students to do the same. We simply established the following ground rules to ensure that the use of water bottles did not become disruptive.

- The water bottle had to be clear and contain only water.
- Toys were not allowed in class. If the student played with the bottle, it was then considered a toy and taken away.
- Students without water bottles, for whatever reason, could still get drinks from the water fountains at appropriate times.
- As much as possible, bathroom breaks would still be taken at recess times or during independent work times.
- If condensation was dripping off the water bottle, the student was responsible for placing tissue or paper towels under the bottle to prevent work on the desk from getting wet.

Results: These water guidelines became virtually unnecessary after two or three days. Students did not play with the water bottles or misuse them. The use of restrooms did not dramatically increase. Students really did seem more alert; the water perked them up or provided that momentary break from paying attention that brains need. In sharing this practice with colleagues at my school or at presentations, teachers and administrators expressed concern about the potential distraction the bottles would cause and the additional time the students would spend using the bathroom. My response is that you simply must give it a try to see how trouble-free it is and how well it works. Incidentally, I have also found that, at slow-moving committee meetings, I now rely heavily on my water to perk me up.

■ ■ ■

Sleep

Adequate sleep is absolutely necessary for efficient functioning of the human brain. It is during particular sleep cycles that information is organized and transferred from short-term memory into long-term memory (Sylwester, 1995). Two-thirds of all adults need between six and a half and eight and a half hours of sleep. Children need even more. People sleep in cycles of approximately 90 minutes. If a person sleeps eight full hours, yet is wakened in the middle of a sleep cycle, he or she will probably feel more tired than a person sleeping only six hours but ending the slumber between cycles (Howard, 2000). However, during each cycle, a period of time exists where memory is affected. When a person sleeps just six hours, he or she is deprived of one cycle and, therefore, something learned or encountered that day will not be transferred to long-term memory. When a person loses many hours of sleep, especially over several days, learning can be considerably affected.

Young children, up until about the age of 11, naturally go to sleep early and wake up early. They are ready to start school at around 7:30 a.m., but most elementary schools begin closer to 8:30 or 9:00 a.m. From the ages of 12 through about 17, students' bodies, due to hormonal chemicals, are programmed to go to sleep later and wake up later. Most secondary schools begin their day around 7:30 a.m., but adolescents are generally not completely alert until closer to 9:00 a.m. By rising so early, these students have missed sleep cycles and, therefore, retain less information taken in by the brain on the previous day (Sousa, 1995). They may also be simply tired because they have had less than the required number of hours of sleep their bodies require to feel fully rested. Consequently, these students will not pay full attention during lessons and may even fall asleep in class. A sleeping student is certainly not learning valuable, new information. It would seem that school districts allow afterschool sports and bus schedules to dictate their schools' beginning and ending times rather than the students' brains and learning.

Movement

Movement helps students learn in several ways. When someone says he thinks better on his feet, he probably really does. Just standing up can increase the blood flow in the human body, bringing more oxygen to the brain. The increased oxygen gives the brain more energy and reduces stress, and it promotes the production of hormones that enhance the growth and strengthen the connections between the brain cells. Sitting for extended periods of time can have detrimental effects on the body, including reduced deep breathing, increased pressure on the spine, and strained eyes (Jensen, 2000). Students who are required to stand or move around during a lesson have less physical fatigue and therefore concentrate more efficiently on the concepts or tasks at hand.

Neuroscientists have discovered that the brain's cerebellum, involved in most learning, operates at high capacity during times of movement. One Canadian study found that of 500 students, those who spent one extra hour per day in a physical education class scored higher on examinations than did those who did not have increased movement. The results also showed that with participation in frequent aerobic exercise, the students increased their reaction time, creativity, and short-term memory (Sylwester, 1995). Other studies have shown that people who exercise regularly (about 45 minutes three times per week or more) seem to grow more dendrite connections between brain cells and have faster recall and reactions. People who do not exercise, or very rarely and sporadically exercise, have a higher rate of depression than those who get regular aerobic exercise (Howard, 2000). Establishing the routine of physical exercise is important for our youth, especially in a time where screens (TV, computer, and video game) seem to monopolize so much of their time.

Exercise is not the only movement that affects students' learning. Movement in terms of changing locations can also cause a marked improvement in memory. If a student sits in the same desk in the same position in the room day after day, his or her learning is tied to that one location. No particular memory trigger is built into this scenario. Do you remember exactly where you learned the definition of a verb? Probably not. Students' memories can be improved when they move to a different location to learn something new. If a teacher introduces a new topic outside or teaches an important skill sitting on the floor, an internal memory trigger will be developed. A teacher can then trigger students' recall by saying, "Remember, we learned about that out by the birch tree." "Remember, you learned about that while you were sitting in your desk" does not generate quite the same spark!

■ ■ ■

EXAMPLE: MOVEMENT IN MATH LESSONS
GRADE 2 AND CLASS FOR THE COGNITIVELY DISABLED

Purpose: To infuse movement into everyday lessons, increasing attention, energy, and memory.

Activity Sample 1: Mr. Tucker, a 2nd grade teacher, finds it useful to keep a small beanbag in each student's desk. As a transition from one academic area to another, he may have the students stand up, with beanbag in hand, for a quick warm-up. The students may gently toss their beanbag from one hand to the other as he or a designated student models for the rest of the class; it may be back and forth in front of the stomach, it may be up higher, arching over the head, or it may be tossed under one leg to the other hand. After a minute or so of this exercise, the students' blood is flowing, and the brain is ready for a new lesson. The beanbags are put away, and instruction begins.

These beanbags may resurface in Mr. Tucker's classroom during an actual lesson as well. During a math lesson when the 2nd graders are to practice counting aloud by 2s, 5s, and 10s, the teacher has the students toss the beanbag back and forth in rhythm as they say each number. Adding this rhythmic movement more intensely displays the counting pattern for the students' brains.

Activity Sample 2: A simple 10-inch ball or a small trampoline is also an effective teaching tool. A teacher of the cognitively disabled, Miss Wiedmeyer was observed teaching a math lesson to a 6-year-old autistic student. Ashley was able to rote count from 1 to 20. However, when attempting one-to-one correspondence counting with small counters at the table, Ashley had trouble. The teacher changed the lesson by holding Ashley's hands as she jumped on a mini-trampoline and counted each bounce aloud. Miss Wiedmeyer also had Ashley play catch with her, counting aloud each time the big rubber ball was tossed back and forth. Not only did these activities help make the one-to-one correspondence counting more concrete, but they also added movement to the lesson. This is particularly important for this autistic child, whose body is in almost constant motion anyway. By guiding Ashley's movements into a particular exercise, Miss Wiedmeyer channeled Ashley's energy and motion into a useful learning activity.

EXAMPLE: STRETCHING IN CLASSROOMS
ALL GRADE LEVELS

Purpose: To improve students' attention through increasing blood flow in the body and to the brain.

Procedures: I remember, when I was a 13-year-old student, rolling my eyes at my friends when Mr. Monarski would make us stand up and do stretching exercises in the middle of class. We thought it was foolish and probably done only to keep old Mr. Monarski himself awake. (He was considered an old man at the time, although I now realize he was probably only 45 or so.) Also, in hindsight, I realize that Mr. Monarski was probably ahead of his time in understanding the role of movement and blood flow in keeping the brain alert for learning. Simple stretching exercises during or between lessons, especially cross-lateral stretches (reaching across the body's midpoint to the other side), will get both of the brain's hemispheres circulating with oxygen-filled blood (Jensen, 2000).

EXAMPLE: STANDING WITHIN LESSONS
GRADE 1

Purpose: To maintain students' attention during a long lesson.

Reasoning: When teachers require that students sit still for too long in their desks (under the guise of paying close attention) they are misunderstanding the attention span of children. The rough rule of thumb is that a person can pay attention to one thing for about the same number of minutes as his or her age. Adults remain 20 years old under this rule of thumb because that is the time limit of their attention in minutes, regardless of their age beyond 20. Although students may sit passively, gazing straight ahead for more than 5, 8, or 11 minutes at a time, their brains are shifting to a different thought even though they appear to be listening to the teacher. All a teacher has to do is shift the modality of the learning briefly now and then to retain the students' attention. The brain is going to shift attention anyway, so the teacher might as well be the one to cause the shift toward something academic rather than the brain shifting to the noise in the hallway or a neighbor's barking dog.

Procedure: During a class discussion, Ms. Fitzsimmons noticed her 1st graders losing their attentiveness. Rather than continuing the discussion by asking the students to raise their hands to be recognized as they had been doing for 5 or 10 minutes, she had the students stand up when they wanted a turn to talk. This change refocused the students' attention and re-engaged them in the discussion for the last five minutes of the lesson.

EXAMPLE: CHANGE OF LOCATION FOR INSTRUCTION
GRADE 3, SCIENCE

Purpose: To increase students' memory and recall.

Procedure: When I taught 3rd grade science, I introduced the pond life unit in the school's library with a video. I taught a lesson introducing inertia in the hallway. And I introduced the concept of chlorophyll outside in the schoolyard. All of these lessons could have easily taken place in my classroom with the students sitting in their desks. However, changing the location for instruction periodically provides the students with a memory trigger for their learning.

EXAMPLE: MOVEMENT IN TAKING A QUIZ
GRADES 6 AND 7, SOCIAL STUDIES

Purpose: To improve students' interest and achievement on a quiz.

Background: Mrs. St. Peter's students performed horribly on a social studies quiz. Their written responses to the questions were dull and short, with little detail to show what they had learned about the topic. The next day, she told her 6th and 7th graders that they would take the quiz again in a different format.

Procedures: Although she did not give them any additional time to study, she did tell them she was looking for more interesting, detailed answers. She also had written the quiz questions on neon-colored note cards considered "cool" by the students, and she had spread them out around the room. Rather than sitting at their desks to complete another quiz paper, the students used their own paper and clipboards to answer the questions placed around the room. The students roved around the room, answering the same quiz questions from the day before, but now they were on their feet, thinking this was a pretty nifty way to take a quiz.

Results: On the second round of quizzes, Mrs. St. Peter found the responses to the quiz questions to be longer and more interesting. Was this due to the fact that she plainly told them to make their answers more detailed and interesting? Was it due to the fact that they were up on their feet and having more fun taking the quiz? Was it due to the fact that they were roaming around the room so close to each other's clipboards they were looking at each other's good answers? We do not know for certain the answers to these questions. However, we do know that the students performed better, and at least reviewed the material a second time, possibly learning more. In the case of this particular quiz and lesson, that additional learning was more important to Mrs. St. Peter than knowing why they performed better.

■ ■ ■

The Body and the Brain

In order to be thoroughly effective, teachers should first be knowledgeable about the brain and learning. The body and brain work in conjunction, and therefore, part of knowing about learning involves understanding the cause and effect of different physical elements on the body and brain. The types and amounts of food, oxygen, and water entering the body affect students' brains and, therefore, their learning. The types and amounts of physical movement and sleep also affect students' brains and their ability to learn. When the body and brain are in optimum physical condition, well rested, well fed, alert, and active, the learner will benefit from more clear understanding and longer-lasting memory of the concepts (Jensen, 2000; Howard, 2000; Sousa, 1995). In addition, active, movement-oriented lessons are fun for the students.

As you teach your next lessons, ask yourself if your students' bodies and brains are in the optimal condition for learning. Ask yourself if there is anything you can do to improve your lessons or improve your students' physical condition to help them learn. Ask yourself if YOU are in the best physical condition for teaching: well rested, well fed, alert, and active. Right now, take a break from reading this book. Take a deep breath, stand up and stretch, drink some water, maybe even take a nap—you just might feel more capable of learning.

Implementing Relevant Brain-Compatible Ideas

Food Tips
- Teach students and parents about proper nutrition for the brain.
- Allow time for a healthy snack for students of all ages in the morning and afternoon.
- Begin a school-based breakfast program, if not daily, at least during high-stakes testing periods.

Oxygen Tips
- Place plants in classrooms to increase amount of oxygen. NASA research shows that dracaena, ficus, and chrysanthemums give off relatively large amounts of oxygen (Jensen, 1998).
- Open classroom windows whenever possible.

Water Tips
- Allow students to keep water bottles at their desks for frequent drinks.
- Drink water yourself to keep alert and to decrease stress.

Sleep Tips
- Flip-flop starting times in school districts for primary and secondary schools. If that is not possible, try to arrange for secondary students to have their core academics after 9:00 a.m.
- Inform parents of the importance of eight full hours of sleep for their children; missed sleep cycles equal missed transfer of learning into long-term memory.

Movement Tips
- Provide opportunities for frequent movement throughout the school day: physical education classes, active lessons, standing, stretching exercises, and so on.
- Change the location of lessons to provide more vivid memory triggers.

4

Relevant Content
and Student Choices

THE BRAIN REMEMBERS INFORMATION THAT IS MEANINGFUL AND LINKED TO PRIOR knowledge or experience. The brain wants to know that new information is important and will be used in the future (McGeehan, 1999). Teachers find students of any age more eager to pay attention and learn when the lesson content is of interest or relevant to them. Therefore, teachers are challenged to make new information interesting to the students and to demonstrate how that information is relevant now or will be in the future.

Making Content Relevant

Some content is so relevant we cannot forget it even if we wanted to. Your own name, for example, is awfully important to you—it would be hard to forget. Other information of life-or-death consequence is quite relevant as well. Once a child learns that fire can be deadly, reminders to leave a burning building are not often needed. However, the vast majority of information does not hold the same degree of relevance or interest to students. The teacher's goal then becomes to prove the significance of a lesson's content in the students' minds in one of two ways—by using instructional strategies that make the skills so interesting that they can't help but learn it, or by proving its immediate or future use so they feel the need to learn that knowledge or skill.

Using Interesting Instructional Strategies

Hundreds of instructional strategies and ideas exist to making learning fun and interesting. Here are just a few:

1. Provide students with choices in their learning.

2. Use a variety of learning and teaching styles during instruction. In a typical class, 46 percent of students are visual learners, 35 percent are kinesthetic learners, and 19 percent are auditory learners (Sousa, 1998). Work at least two of these modalities into each lesson. For example, for each story they hear, show a picture or a chart. For each experiment they perform, have them write down the results. For each graph they study, have them discuss their hypotheses.

3. Hands-on, active learning is innately more interesting and fun. Use it frequently in every academic subject area.

4. Use discovery learning. Don't give the students the answers, but rather provide them with questions. When students can find and manipulate information themselves, they gain ownership of the information.

5. Infuse some surprise, humor, or spontaneity into the instruction periodically to make a point. Breaking into song during instruction comes to mind. Or to introduce a science unit on weather, for instance, enter the room wearing galoshes and a raincoat—you will definitely trigger interest.

6. Don't talk so much. When the predominant sound in a classroom is a teacher's voice, it often indicates the teacher is in too much control of the learning. Students will not maintain interest in the teacher's voice if that is all they ever hear.

7. Purposefully plan your wording of directions. For example, instead of telling a class, "Today you will read the reasons for the fall of the Roman Empire," spark more interest with, "Today you will be detectives searching for clues as to why the Roman Empire fell."

Demonstrating Immediate and Future Use of Lesson Content

It is not uncommon for teachers to hear students ask in a whiny voice, "When are we eeeeeever going to use this?" even if the students don't really want a response. In contrast, one of my 3rd grade math students, Keegan, asked me the same question several times and anxiously waited for a genuine answer. Her question forced me to prove the relevance of the particular math skill. Keegan would nod her head to indicate she accepted my explanation, and the lesson would proceed. Keegan prompted me to begin regularly identifying the immediate relevance and the possible future use of my lessons. Sometimes I would simply state its application. Other times I would have the students brainstorm to help them draw their own conclusions about the lesson's relevance and future application.

In order for students to exert maximum effort, they need to understand that the work being completed and the information being studied are meaningful. The older the student, the more critical this becomes. Because, for better or for worse, as we age we naturally become more skeptical. A young child will learn just for the sake of learning. Secondary students and adults are not nearly as open-minded when it comes to dedicating precious time and effort to learning new information. They think, "If this is useless, why waste my time?" And beyond obtaining more effort from students through meaningful lessons, the brain needs this relevance to learn efficiently. The brain uses relevance in connecting each bit of new knowledge to previously learned information. A stand-alone neuron (brain cell) holding a tidbit of information does the brain little good. It is when that neuron connects to another neuron, and that one to another neuron, and so on, that the connections and learning take place (Sousa, 1995). A fitting metaphor for this process is the letters of the alphabet. One printed letter alone does not mean much. But connected to a sound, it becomes a symbol. And then connections to other letters with sounds result in a whole word that makes sense. Words connected to other words make a sentence of even more meaning. Pretty soon, we have volumes of text full of meaningful information.

Chunking and networking are terms used to describe how the brain groups similar information for meaning and memory. People use chunking, or grouping, regularly to make information useful and manageable to remember (Sousa, 1995). For example, the following set of numbers would be difficult to remember: 8675309. However, by grouping the numbers differently, 867-5309, it becomes more meaningful to us because we recognize it as a phone number, and it is more likely to be remembered.

Networking is the way the brain categorizes information for more efficient memory. To illustrate this categorization, imagine a zoologist who has a cabinet full of files, one for each animal. If haphazardly arranged, it could take hours to find the "tiger" file. But, if the files are organized by class or species, she could look under "felines" to find the "tiger" file quite quickly. Or, if they were organized alphabetically, she would simply find the desired file under "T." The brain works in similar ways. When a youngster learns the term "tiger," he or she will connect that new information to previous knowledge of animals, or perhaps furry animals, or even more specifically, catlike animals. The new term "tiger" is networked in the brain in the "animal" or "cat" file. The brain is inundated with information, so it must screen for meaning and then organize the information accordingly (Wolfe, 2001). If the information is not meaningful or relevant, the brain sees no reason to remember the information and dismisses it.

Knowing how the brain chunks and categorizes information is useful to teachers in helping students connect new information to prior knowledge. For instance, demonstrating how the new skill of multiplication is related to the previously learned concept of addition can make it easier for the students' brains to make connections and learn the new concept. An important thing for teachers to keep in mind is that one student's brain may chunk or categorize information differently from another student's brain. The teacher may think it is most appropriate to group "tiger" under "felines" in that file cabinet, while the student is thinking in alphabetical terms. Both are logical. Brains work logically, but like fingerprints, they are unique. Everyone has had diverse life experiences and varying background knowledge upon which to build. To account for these differences, teachers should often use diverse examples, metaphors, and pictures to increase the chance of the information being relevant to every student.

One way to minimize these experiential differences between students is to provide as many real-life, authentic experiences as possible. Using the tiger example again, one student in a class may have only seen a tiger in a cartoon picture, while another may have actually been on an African safari to see tigers in the wild. If you take the class on a field trip to the zoo, the students will share the common experience of seeing a tiger. This experience can be used to facilitate discussion and activities in the classroom. Logistically, teachers cannot provide daily field trips all over the world to provide extensive background knowledge. But that does not mean we must only rely on textbooks. Certainly, textbooks provide important, useful information, but they do not provide experiences. Students need a balance of both. In addition to field trips, teachers can provide experiential learning by regularly using hands-on activities, simulations, Web sites, models, experiments, and guest speakers.

■ ■ ■

EXAMPLE: DISCOVERY LEARNING—MAKING MODEL BRIDGES
UPPER PRIMARY OR SECONDARY LEVEL

Purpose: To implement hands-on discovery learning in the classroom.

Background: Active modes of learning provide students the opportunity to make their own discoveries. New information becomes more interesting and relevant to students if they want or need to know it and when they have ownership in discovering the answers and applying the new knowledge.

Lesson: A student can read in a textbook or be told by the teacher whether a suspension bridge or an arch bridge would be better able to withstand heavy weight and difficult weather conditions. That information is likely to go in one ear and out the other if the student doesn't care about bridges or has no use for the knowledge. To make the subject engaging, one teacher gives pairs of students wooden craft sticks to build models of these two types of bridges, along with a hair dryer to produce wind and blocks to apply weight. The students do research to determine what each bridge looks like. Next, they test their bridges against the elements of weight and wind to discover which bridge is stronger. Graphing the results of an entire class can provide enough information for generalizations and conclusions to be made.

Results: When students are responsible for the discovery of the information and have a purpose and ownership of the information, the odds are they will learn it.

EXAMPLE: K—W—L—U CHART
ANY GRADE LEVEL

Purpose: To improve student learning through reviewing prior knowledge, having choice in what will be learned, reflecting on what was learned, and contemplating the immediate and future application of the new knowledge.

Procedures: Many teachers know about and use "Know—Want to know—Learned" (KWL) charts. This is a practice in which the teacher or the students, at the start of a lesson or even a longer unit experience, begin a chart listing what they already know about the topic and what they want to learn about that topic. Prior to the lesson, or series of lessons in a unit, this establishes the background knowledge of the students and develops ownership in the learning by soliciting students' desires as to new knowledge they wish to gain. At the end of the lesson or unit, the students then spend some time reflecting on and recording what they actually learned. All three of these activities are extremely brain-compatible and effective teaching and learning practices.

To make the KWL strategy even stronger, I add a "**U**" to the chart for "**Use**," to heighten meaning and relevance. I want the students to ponder how will they use the new knowledge learned in the lesson or unit, both immediately and in their futures.

Results: An end result of adding the "U" is helping students routinely think about how to apply knowledge, which is good. A word of warning though—a sometimes not-so-good result is the students' routine of asking me how they would use almost everything I taught. Sometimes, I could not come up with an answer, causing me to become frustrated with particular strands of curriculum. What I would tell the students, however, was that I personally have not used it yet in my boring life, and maybe I am not even smart enough to know how and when it will be used. They seemed to like the challenge of perhaps being smarter than the teacher by trying to predict a use for it in their lives. Soon, they were talking themselves into how important the information was to know.

■ ■ ■

The Value of Student Choice

Learning becomes more meaningful and relevant if students can have choices in what they study, the work they do, and how their school functions. If your students were offered a choice of what to do for the entire six hours of their school day, what would they choose? Recess? Lunch? Physical education, perhaps? If given their choice of anything to learn about in school, what would they choose? Baseball card facts or video game strategies? These are exactly the reasons why educators cannot and do not allow *free* choice of options for their students. However, offering appropriate choices in school, within allowable parameters, is an extremely powerful way to facilitate meaningful, relevant learning and a collaborative climate.

When a student feels some control over the learning process, a wider range of learning, both rote and meaningful, occurs. Under these circumstances, the brain's cortex is more fully functional. The cortex manages higher-level, more meaningful thinking processes, including problem solving, creativity, critical thinking, analysis, synthesis, and decision making. When the student feels the learning is solely controlled by the teacher, the learning that occurs is likely to be only simple and rote in nature. Under these circumstances, similar to when students are under stress or duress, the cortex essentially shuts down, and the brain's limbic system predominates. The limbic system manages simple skills based on survival or instincts and routines (Caine & Caine, 1994). When some control and choices are provided for students, the content relevance is increased, their interest is heightened, stress is reduced, learning styles and ability levels are better accounted for, and both motivation and effort are enhanced.

Effective Choices for Research Projects

Most educators have a predetermined curriculum that must be completed within each grade level. Therefore, we cannot let students choose the curriculum we teach. Yet within the specified curriculum, a student can be allowed a variety of choices. Having choices in learning allows the student to begin with the positive emotional state associated with doing what he or she wants to do (McGeehan, 1999). This feeling of ownership of learning produces less ambivalence during the lessons. When students are allowed to choose a particular topic to research, for example, suddenly most of what they discover is relevant and interesting. Students become much like sponges, soaking up all the information they can find on their topic.

■ ■ ■

EXAMPLE: RESEARCH PROJECT
GRADES 3 THROUGH 6, SOCIAL STUDIES

Purpose: To provide students with choice in learning and to allow them to work within different multiple intelligences.

Background: One of the best teaching practices I ever incorporated into regular practice was to have my students complete an independent research project during each of the social studies and science units taught during the school year. As just one segment in a month-long unit, these research projects usually resulted in more learning than any lecture I ever gave and always resulted in motivated, actively engaged students.

Procedures: I provide the class with a list of approximately a dozen project choices, with the last one always being "Develop your own project, but get the teacher's approval before starting your work." (These 3rd graders typically came up with more creative project ideas than their teacher.) When forming my list of project ideas, I made sure to incorporate different learning styles and multiple intelligences within the options. For example, within a desert unit, the project choices may include the following:

• Write and illustrate an alphabet book about the desert. Choose an animal, plant, or land formation for each letter of the alphabet. Make a page for each topic and include your research and a picture.

• Develop a song about the desert using a familiar tune. Your song must include true facts that you learned in your research. You may write your song on paper to read or sing aloud or ask your teacher about using the overhead projector to display your song so we can all sing along.

- Make a poster about ecological issues in the desert. Tell the class about the issues you uncovered in your research.

- Construct a model or diorama depicting life in the desert for the plants or animals or both. Be prepared to tell the class information about each item you included in your project.

- Compare and contrast desert plants with common house-plants. You may bring in examples to show the class, or use our classroom plants during your presentation. Your research and ideas may be displayed on a poster with a Venn diagram or explained in a written report.

- Pretend you are one particular desert animal. Write a creative story about your life in the desert. Include true facts from your research describing your adaptations for living there and other facts about you. Also tell what you like about living in the desert and what you don't like. You may read your story or act it out as a play.

- Show or make a map of the world's five main deserts. Research the climate of each and develop charts or graphs to compare each of their annual rainfall averages, temperature averages for day and night, size in square miles, etc.

- Develop your own fabulous project idea! Get the teacher's approval before you start working.

To begin implementation of project-based learning, I send a letter home to parents at the beginning of each unit informing them of their child's research assignment along with the list of the project choices. Parents are advised that approximately three class periods will be used to complete the work, but if additional time becomes necessary, it must be done as homework. I let them know that their child may make use of many supplies available at school, but some special items required for a particular project may need to be brought from home. The parents and students are also told that I assess the research project in the following four areas: the research, the physical project itself, the effort put forth, and the presentation of the project to the class.

The presentations are as beneficial as the research completed by the students. Each student has a turn in front of the class to share his or her new knowledge and exhibit the project. The students are typically hesitant at the beginning of the year to speak in front of the class. Before long, though, they consider it a routine practice, and it becomes difficult to limit their presentations to the designated time allotment. The classmates often become so interested in each other's projects that, following a presentation, questions from the audience can go on and on and on. I learned to tell the students that each presenter would answer only two questions from the audience. It is interesting to see that some students ask questions related to information presented so they could learn more about the topic, while other students' questions are procedural in nature, such as how many sources were used or how the physical project had been constructed.

Results: Students are highly motivated because they are able to choose a topic of high interest within the established parameters and because they are able to be the expert in sharing their knowledge with peers. This accountability seems to encourage them to increase the time and effort in their work. The project choices also allow the students to work within their preferred intelligence or learning style. And every student, regardless of ability level, is able to research, learn, and create an end-product masterpiece. Both the brightest gifted child in the class and the student with the most severe learning disabilities manage to accomplish the assignment, even if they happened to choose the same project option. For example, a high-level alphabet book developed by one student included lengthy paragraphs and beautiful drawings on each page. Another student chose the same alphabet book project idea and did her best with one brief sentence of research per page and pictures from magazines as illustrations. Both students felt successful in their learning and had something unique to share with the class.

■ ■ ■

Effective Choices in Learning

The brain remembers what is meaningful. Long-term memory is increased, therefore, when a student

- Is interested in a particular topic.
- Is enthused to learn as much as possible.
- Can put the information or skill to use in his or her own life.
- Has choices in both how to learn the material as well as how to demonstrate this new knowledge.

Success in learning is heightened when a student learns through his or her preferred learning style or multiple intelligences. Additionally, throughout the learning process the teacher can more thoroughly evaluate the students' understanding of concepts and skills if assessments are used that capitalize on each individual's different learning styles.

Teachers can learn more about multiple intelligences theory through the work of Howard Gardner (1983) and other authors. The basic premise is that people have areas of natural strength or preference in the way they learn and use concepts and skills. Howard Gardner's recognized intelligences are

- Linguistic
- Logical-Mathematical
- Spatial
- Bodily-Kinesthetic
- Musical
- Interpersonal
- Intrapersonal
- Naturalist

Once the educator understands learning through different learning styles and multiple intelligences, he or she can use that information in lesson planning to provide a variety of instructional practices to meet the differing needs and preferences of students. Even more powerful may be the process of teaching the students about each of the different intelligences or areas of strength that people have. Using the following child-friendly terms for the multiple intelligences may help even the youngest students' comprehend this idea (Armstrong, 1994):

- Word-smart
- Number-smart
- Picture-smart
- Body-smart
- Music-smart
- People-smart
- Self-smart
- Nature-smart

Prior to weaving the multiple intelligences into everyday lessons, teachers may wish to set up multiple intelligence learning centers around the classroom. The students will have the opportunity to explore and experience tasks corresponding to each of the eight categories. See Figure 4.1 for sample learning center tasks.

Helping students discover their own personal strong and weak areas within the multiple intelligences is beneficial in a variety of ways. It will help students understand that they are all very capable of learning in one way or another. This can be a huge self-esteem builder for a student who considers him or herself a failure or even "dumb" because he or she could not seem to do well in certain classes. Perhaps a student will discover, for example, that when trying to show knowledge through writing answers on a test, he fails miserably. However, if given the option to express his knowledge on the same content material by making a model and verbally explaining the information, he can perform very effectively.

Teaching students to recognize their preferred learning styles or intelligences also helps them in making good choices during their learning. When offered a variety of project options in a class, each student knows which choice best matches his or her learning strengths. Therefore, he or she is more likely to enjoy the work while maximizing the learning. Teachers and students should also identify the weaker areas of intelligences for individuals and work to strengthen them. While these weaker areas may never be areas of great achievement for the individual, they shouldn't be ignored either. The brain does have some windows of opportunity when, developmentally, it is easier to learn certain tasks. For example, a person can most easily learn to play a musical instrument between the ages of 3 and 10 years old. If we dismiss any musical ability in a child during that age period, we may miss an ability that can be developed.

Understanding the strong and weak intelligences in each individual also helps both the teacher and students to make choices about grouping students for learning. Sometimes a teacher may want to cluster students homogenously according to an area of strength. For instance, four or five students who are very logical and mathematical in their thinking may serve to challenge each other to reach new levels in that area. Their end result may be a high-level, specialized project or report. On the other hand, teachers may wish to group students heterogeneously so that students with different strengths and weaknesses are working together. This combination may promote cooperation and teamwork, and may help

FIGURE 4.1

Multiple Intelligences Learning Center Tasks

Multiple Intelligence Category	Student Tasks
Verbal-Linguistic (Word-Smart)	• Write a bumper sticker or slogan about your school. • Tell a joke, tall tale, or tongue twister. • Make as many sentences as you can by recombining the words in this sentence. • Pass a story around and add to it.
Math-Logic (Number-Smart)	• Listen to two types of music and compare and contrast. • Calculate: $50 + 30 - 12 =$ • Create categories and sort math terms into groups. • Develop a pattern out of a collection of objects.
Visual-Spatial (Picture-Smart)	• Line up by height without talking. • Draw a picture of your favorite story setting. • Show a partner how to read a map. • Pair up, then take turns drawing the same picture. • Find hidden images in pictures or clouds. • Draw your dream house.
Bodily-Kinesthetic (Body-Smart)	• Learn a dance. • Talk in sign language—real or your own made-up version. • Play charades. • Do 10 jumping jacks and touch your toes 5 times. • With a partner, use your bodies to form letters of the alphabet. • Demonstrate an athletic skill you are good at.
Musical (Music-Smart)	• Play a rhythm on a drum and have a partner repeat it. • Move streamers to music. • Create a song, rap, or jingle. • Play "name that tune" with a partner. • Listen to music and rate it. • Hum or sing a song.
Interpersonal (People-Smart)	• Tell about something of interest to you. • Tell a joke to a friend. • Talk about methods of expressing encouragement to others. • Read aloud a poem with a partner. • Share secrets with a friend. • Guess a partner's emotions from facial expressions and body language.

(continued)

FIGURE 4.1 (continued)

Multiple Intelligences Learning Center Tasks

Multiple Intelligence Category	Student Tasks
Intrapersonal (Self-Smart)	• Tell about something creative you have done. • Make a wish. • Think about your personal strengths and weaknesses. • Fill out a survey on your likes and dislikes. • Define one of these words: trust, honor, justice, peace. • Tell about an improvement skill you would like to learn. • Write a diary entry.
Naturalist (Nature-Smart)	• Use magazine pictures to classify animals according to common characteristics. • Compare and contrast animals' survival adaptations. • Listen and list all sounds of nature heard. • Imagine a new plant species—write or tell about it. • Debate over using the natural resources in a rain forest. • Make a conservation poster.

---

students to recognize and value differences. Each child can feel like the group's expert in at least one area. The end product in this case might result in a very interesting work of synergy, where the resulting product in its entirety is worth much more than the separate contributions.

■ ■ ■

EXAMPLE: COOPERATIVE GROUP ASSIGNMENT
GRADES 4 THROUGH 7, SCIENCE

Purpose: To provide students the opportunity to improve both academic and social skills through working in small groups.

Lesson: In one classroom, students had been randomly divided into four groups. The reading assignment from the science book dealt with the four ways ponds could form. Being a rather dry topic (no pun intended!), the teacher decided to add interest to the lesson by asking each group to research only one of the ways a pond forms. Each group would then teach their information to the rest of the class. (The lesson turned out to be a huge success.)

We know from the work of William Glasser (1998) and others that what we teach others we truly learn ourselves. With this in mind, the teacher knew that each child would thoroughly learn at least one of the four pond-forming methods. These groups of 5th graders instinctively applied their multiple intelligence strength areas for methods of teaching others. One group used charades to act out a beaver chewing down a tree, which blocked a river's flow and formed a pond. Another group simply read aloud from the book and displayed pictures drawn on poster board to accompany the explanation. A third group had one member explain their pond-forming method while two other group members simultaneously sketched that process on the board. The last group wrote a rap and sang their song explaining how a pond formed. The rap was complete with props and "cool" sound effects.

Results: Did this group learning take more work on the teacher's part? No, because the kids designed the lessons and taught each other. Did it take more time for the lesson than simply reading the textbook? Yes, absolutely. But did the students learn more than simply reading the textbook? Yes, absolutely.

Effective Choices for Assessment

Offering choices within assessment or testing is within the realm of possibilities. It can be extremely beneficial to the student and to the teacher who really wants to know what and how much the student has learned. Because a student will learn best through a preferred intelligence or learning style, it is logical to allow the student to demonstrate new knowledge through a preferred intelligence or learning style as well. This does not need to be a lot of extra work for the teacher.

■ ■ ■

EXAMPLE: DIFFERENTIATING ASSESSMENT
GRADES 3 THROUGH 7, LITERATURE

Purpose: To provide choice to students in assessment methods, which allows the teacher to discover the students' actual understanding and knowledge.

Procedures: One 7th grade teacher used a method of student choice to assess her students' comprehension of a trade book. Occasionally, the students in the class would "buddy-read" a chapter of the book during class time; the students would take turns reading aloud to each other until the chapter was finished. The teacher could walk around the room and know for certain that the students were reading and, with some simple questioning, ascertain if they comprehended what they were reading. However, the majority of the book's chapters were assigned for reading outside of the class period. She was then more skeptical about the depth of comprehension of the story, or even if it was being read at all. As a means of fluent, consistent assessment, she had the students write in their journals almost daily about what had been read. She found that by offering a few choices of question prompts, most of the children did well writing about the chapter they had read the previous night. Several of the students, however, were weak writers. They were, therefore, being evaluated as if they did not comprehend what they had read. In reality, they just weren't taking the time or putting the effort into writing down all they knew.

The teacher decided to change her assessment format by allowing students to choose to answer prompts in their journals as usual or answer the same prompts verbally with the teacher. Each student choosing this new option only needed approximately three minutes to discuss his or her reading. Those poor writers, given the chance to explain using their verbal skills, could more accurately prove the degree to which they comprehended their reading on a daily basis.

Student Sample: Student X is a weak writer but strong verbally. Notice the difference between her written response and verbal response when permitted to talk to the teacher about her reading. If the student had only allowed to respond with written journal responses, the teacher may have assumed she only had a simplistic level of understanding of the story's content and the characters' actions and feelings. Student X's verbal response gave the teacher a more valid picture of the student's comprehension.

Story Comprehension Prompt—How was the value of Grandma's antique doll changed due to Patricia's action in Chapter 6?

Student X's Written Journal Response: The value changed because the hair didn't look as good after Patricia cut it. The grandma was upset it lost the long brown hair because she always wanted long brown hair but couldn't have it.

Student X's Verbal Response: "The granddaughter in the story, Patricia, cut the grandma's old, antique doll's hair. The grandma had had it since she was a little girl. It was really special to her. When she had been young, she always wanted her hair, that was the same exact color as the doll's hair, to be long, just like the doll's. The grandma's mother, so Patricia's great-grandma, always cut her hair short because she was afraid that long hair would end up with nits in it. Nits are lice, I guess. So when, years later, Patricia cut the doll's hair, even though Grandma was grown up, it still made her feel sad to see her favorite old doll with short hair like she was always stuck with. So, the doll lost value for Grandma. It maybe even lost value, money, as an antique because when Patricia cut its hair, it probably ended up looking pretty messy or ugly too."

Example: Aligning Assessment to Classroom Instruction *Grades 2 Through 12*

Purpose: To allow students choice in portions of tests so that they can show their understanding and knowledge through their strongest learning styles.

Procedures: Another approach to assessment uses similar choices in an end-of-unit testing procedure in a science unit. It did not match classroom instruction to evaluate students solely from a written test supplied by the textbook company when so much of the rest of the instruction during the course of the unit had included hands-on learning. So I developed my own end-of-unit assessment using the textbook test as a starting point. Each student was required to complete at least a portion of a written test because I believe it is important that students learn to express their knowledge in writing. Portions of the test were also developed that could be answered in the typical written format, a verbal format, or a drawing format. The choice was left up to the students. The students who were more verbal took turns coming up to my desk to describe particular science concepts or processes, while other students worked at their desks to explain these same concepts in writing. Still others chose to draw the science concepts and use arrows and words to label their sketches. Each of these three sets of responses was evaluated on the same criteria—the student's ability to use key vocabulary accurately.

Results: It was stunning for me to discover how much a few students knew when they could tell me or draw to show what they knew. I would never have known this had they been required to write all answers. This new method did not require lots of extra time or work on my part as the teacher; it was just a matter of getting in the habit of thinking differently about tests. The students found the tests less threatening and more appealing to take, and they seemed to have more confidence and pride in proving their knowledge.

■ ■ ■

Involving Students in Decision Making

Choices in school can extend beyond the actual classroom learning and lessons. It is beneficial for students to have some choice and decision-making power within the classroom and school environment. Within a classroom, students should have input in developing expectations or rules and in deciding on potential positive and negative consequences. Although the teacher has the final say in the class rules, asking for input from the students makes them feel ownership for their environment. Even the physical classroom environment can hold choices for the students. Students can be involved in deciding such things as where the reading corner should be, whether desks should be in rows or groups for the next month, and how the hallway bulletin board related to a new math unit should be designed.

Teachers should certainly give guidelines for students' decisions, and, quite honestly, sometimes strongly guide the students' choices toward what the teacher intends. Even in a somewhat contrived decision-making opportunity, the students can still be made to feel that they are important and have a voice in the matter. Think about a parent allowing a child to choose his or her own clothes to wear for the day. Depending on the age of the child, the parent may end up horrified to be out in public with the child's choice of outfit if the child is given free choice of everything in the closet. Sometimes it is better for the adult to offer a couple of options from which the child can decide, such as, "Do you prefer the red shirt or the blue shirt today?" The child still feels some control over the choice, but the parent doesn't have to look at a combination of a striped shirt and flowered pants all day. Similarly, teachers can offer choices for students while still ensuring that the results remain desirable to the teacher as well.

The operation of a student council within a school, even a primary school, is a good way to foster students' responsibility and decision-making power in the building. Naturally, students cannot be given control to run the school, but a student council provides students with additional choices beyond the classroom walls. Many times the business of student councils tends to be service oriented, which provides admirable role modeling for these students' futures. It can also be a wonderful opportunity for children to identify an issue or problem, brainstorm possible ideas or solutions, choose and follow through on the best choice, and then reflect on or evaluate the results.

■ ■ ■

EXAMPLE: STUDENT VOICE IN SCHOOL POLICIES
GRADE 4, STUDENT COUNCIL ACTION

Purpose: To allow students a voice in developing specific school policies.

Background: A 4th grader wrote a very businesslike letter to her principal regarding the length of the school's lunch period. The student explained in detail why she believed the time allotted for the students to eat was much too short. She took the time to classify her reasons according to the social and health needs of the students and obtained the signatures of about 30 other students who agreed with her.

Procedures: The principal brought this issue to the school's student council for its consideration. The first, and seemingly only, solution, according to the students, was to lengthen the lunch period. The principal explained to the student council members that due to class scheduling, teachers' work hours, and state requirements for instructional minutes within a school week, increasing the lunchtime could not be an option.

However, the students did not admit defeat and give up at this point. Rather, they looked back at the reasons outlined in the student's letter and determined that the most important issues to consider were the student health issues involved. She had stated that rushing to eat so much food was not healthy for digestion. Frequently students did not have the time to finish all their food, so it was being thrown away. She stated not only was this wasteful, but it resulted in students not getting enough nourishment.

Results: After much discussion, the student council arrived at a potential solution to those health issues. They had learned in health class that it was actually healthier to eat small meals throughout the day rather than just the typical two or three large meals. It is also better for the brain's functioning to have healthy snacks during the day. So, the student council concluded that one or two healthy items from each student's sack lunch could be eaten during the morning recess time. This decreased the amount of food to be eaten during the short lunch period, the children got all the same nourishment, and food wasn't wasted. The students who chose the school's hot lunch program were allowed to bring a healthy snack from home for recess time. Some teachers kept a box of crackers on hand for those students who forgot their snacks.

The student council considered potential problems with this idea and only came up with the possible littering of the playground with snack wrappers during the morning recess. The council determined that a wastebasket could be kept in one of the doorways where students exit and enter for recess. A student would be designated to bring that basket outside at the start of recess and back inside when the bell rang. The student council determined the rules and guidelines for this new process, explained them over the public address system to the student body, and informed the students that this snack idea was on probation. If problems arose, it would be discontinued. The students were given a choice and a voice in the functioning of a school and, through problem solving, changed a part of the system to a better way of doing things.

■ ■ ■

Using Choice to Motivate Students

Success breeds success. If we can make a student feel successful in learning and satisfied with life within the classroom and school, he or she will be motivated to continue striving to achieve. Part of making students feel successful is meeting their personal learning needs. When students find school and learning interesting, they want to learn. Making lessons interesting and the content and skills being taught meaningful and relevant to the students is one way of meeting students' needs. Another way to meet the needs of students is through recognizing their individual abilities and learning styles and implementing practices related to those individual differences. Teachers can make learning fun and relevant and, at the same time, allow for individual differences by offering choices to students within their learning practices and school environment. These choices and responsibilities help students learn and grow. We want children to love learning and we want them to love school.

As you recall from Chapter 1, brain-based learning has changed the way teachers make decisions about their classroom practices. As neuro-scientists have discovered more about the brain's functions, educators have gleaned crucial information about how the brain learns. We know the human brain likes interesting activities, relevant knowledge, and choices. Consequently, students do benefit from having meaningful choices in their learning and school environment because when people are allowed to make choices, interest, motivation, and effort are all increased while stress is decreased. As adults, we know it is certainly easier to become enthused about completing a task when it is something we are excited about, when we understand its relevance in our lives, when we have some control over the process—when we have choices. Let's offer our students those same opportunities.

Implementing Relevant Brain-Compatible Ideas

Immediate and Future Use of Lessons' Content Tips
- Use K-W-L-U charts during lessons or units of study.
- Discuss how information learned applies in future careers.
- Point out the direct and indirect links between curricular areas for your students.

Discovery Learning Tips
- Provide experiential, authentic learning opportunities through hands-on learning, simulations, guest speakers, and field trips.
- Pose new information as questions or mysteries so the students can discover the answers.

Student Choices Tips
- Teach students about multiple intelligences and learning styles, and plan lessons to accommodate individual students' needs.
- Use project-based learning regularly to allow for individual choices and to foster research.
- Provide options in differentiated levels or expectations of assignments to account for those who need an extra challenge or have learning difficulties.
- Develop a decision-making process with students, such as a student council.
- Give students some choices regarding the physical room arrangement of desks, bulletin boards, mailboxes, etc.
- Occasionally, have students choose their partners for group work.
- Offer choices of different types of quizzes and assignments aligned with students' learning styles or intelligence areas of strength.

5

Time, Time, and More Time

TIME IS A FOUR-LETTER WORD. THE REASON I POINT THIS OUT IS BECAUSE THE word *time* frequently has a negative connotation similar to those other, naughty, four-letter words we shouldn't say. Time seems to be an issue that people struggle with throughout their lives. We hear, think, or say, "Where has the time gone?" or "I should spend more time with my family" or "I need to spend more time at work" or "I don't have the time right now" or "How am I going to pass the time today?" Is there ever just the perfect balance of time?

Teachers cope with a large number of time-related issues in their careers—from the vast number of minute-to-minute lesson changes to long-term issues like how much preparation time is adequate for high-stakes testing. Most educators feel frustrated because there is simply not enough time . . . to correct assignments, to thoroughly teach one topic before forging ahead into another, to collaborate with colleagues, to take graduate-level coursework, or to even have a 10-minute break during the day.

Time also plays a role in brain-based learning. Some of the news is good, and some of it is of the four-letter-word sort. In a review of an extensive number of brain-related books and articles, the following three topics dealing with time are prevalent:

- Time on Task
- Need for More Time
- Opportune Time Periods for Learning

Each of these topics, like other time issues in our lives, relies on thorough knowledge of the issue and a healthy balance of action.

Time on Task

Time on task is a concept that has changed dramatically in light of new brain research. Traditionally, the students who paid attention for long periods of time were considered the "good" students. Now we find that the human brain is simply not designed for long periods of attentiveness. Those "good" students were probably just good actors who *appeared* to be paying constant attention. The truth is that their minds were probably wandering at least every 20 minutes. Some teachers' expectations for length of time on task for students have been inappropriate and unreasonable. I remember hearing the rule, in an early childhood development course, that a child's attention span is no longer in minutes than their age in years, so a 5-year-old can pay undivided attention to a task for no more than five minutes. I thought this was an exaggeration—until my first position teaching kindergarten. The rule was right on! A few years later, when I moved into a 7th grade teaching position, I was expecting the students to be far more attentive than kindergartners. I was wrong. My unscientific conclusion quickly became that 7th graders revert to the 5-year-old attention span unless the topic is fashion, girls or boys, or cute musicians. Children, and even adults for that matter, cannot keep their minds entirely focused on one item or concept for as long as many teachers desire or believe possible.

Studies have shown that adults in the work place need mental and physical breaks to increase productivity, quality, and morale. Okogbaa and Shell, in *The Measurement of Knowledge Worker Fatigue* (1986), summarize the studies by stating that, as a general rule, workers need 5- to 10-minute breaks every one to two hours. The length and frequency of the breaks should be in accordance with the job being completed and the needs of the worker (Howard, 2000). Attention span studies of children and young adults reveal similar but even more dramatic results. Students need a break in concentration *at least* every 20 minutes. Following a 20-minute period or less, the brain naturally shifts in attention whether we want it to or not (Sousa, 1995). The key for teachers is to realize this and plan for it.

This is not to say that the lesson's topic should change every 20 minutes, but rather the way the students are working with that one topic should change. For example, a teacher has been lecturing for 15 solid minutes on the topic of Benjamin Franklin's inventions. It is likely that many students' brains have shifted from listening to perhaps gazing out the window, thinking about Friday night's football game, or writing a note to a friend. If the teacher shifts his or her actions from lecturing to showing pictures of the inventions, the students' brains are likely to shift along with that new task for the next 10 to 20 minutes. The students are still concentrating on Franklin's inventions, just in a new way. Thoughts of the football game aren't likely to have a chance to enter the mind.

As another example, suppose students are assigned to read silently for a 30-minute block of time. At some point during that time period, their brains shift to thinking about or doing something else. To avoid off-task thoughts and behaviors, the teacher might interrupt and change the activity after 20 minutes. The teacher tells the class to spend the next three minutes discussing what they have just read with a classmate or writing about it in a journal, and then return to silent reading for 10 more minutes. The teacher allows their brains to shift from steady concentration on reading to a new behavior, yet the students are still focusing on the assigned text. And, if truth be known, it is not the end of the world if the students do completely shift their attention to a new topic for a brief amount of time. We have all shifted our attention from the task at hand to daydream, stretch, or get a drink of water. It can give the brain a bit of an intermission to relax and rejuvenate for deeper concentration a minute later.

■ ■ ■

EXAMPLE: TIME ON TASK
GRADE 1 WRITING PROJECT

Purpose: To keep a class of 1st graders meaningfully engaged with a writing project for an hour.

Background: It is very challenging to keep a class of young students on task with any learning activity for an hour-long block of time. It is impossible if the teacher expects the students to actually be writing for an hour. Therefore, Mrs. Brusky used a variety of instructional techniques to keep her students successfully engaged in writing stories about a best friend.

Lesson: The lesson began with a quick review of a story about friendship read the previous day. Mrs. Brusky asked if it was a good story and why. She led them in a 10-minute analysis of the author's success with different story elements using concrete examples from the book such as

• Did the author write a good introduction that got the audience hooked into wanting to learn more?

• Was the ending a good conclusion?

• Did the details in the middle give all the information that the reader wanted to know?

• Did the author use descriptive words?

Mrs. Brusky explained to the students that those story elements should also appear in their own stories about their best friends. She then had the students draw a story web to plan out their ideas. Following that 10-minute exercise, Mrs. Brusky had the students move to a different desk and share ideas from their webs with a partner. After a couple of minutes of discussion, the children could add more to their own web if they had gained any new insights from their partners.

Next, Mrs. Brusky modeled writing a story about her own best friend on an overhead projector. This was the longest portion of the lesson—about 20 minutes. Knowing this would be the longest time period they would have to be mainly listening and watching her work, she motivated them by telling them they had to guess who she was writing about. As she wrote, Mrs. Brusky not only spoke the written words aloud but also explained her thinking about writing. She talked of an exciting introduction, explained her choices for several of her descriptive words, and asked the students for their advice on how to punctuate the end of each sentence. She also made it obvious that she was getting ideas from some writing posters displayed in the classroom. By the end of the model story, the students had figured out that Mrs. Brusky's best friend was Mr. Brusky, and they enthusiastically advised her on how to conclude her story. Prior to having the class read her model story aloud, she had the students stand up, stretch, and then remain standing to do a choral reading.

After approximately 45 minutes of preparation for writing, the students spent the last quarter of the hour independently writing their own stories. Mrs. Brusky reminded them to use the effective story elements they had discussed and incorporate their friendship ideas from their webs. She also passed out little hand-shaped papers with "helping hands" writing tips on each finger. (See Figure 5.1.)

Results: All the students were on task during this lesson because, throughout the hour, Mrs. Brusky had them refocus their attention to new activities. Although the topic never changed, the students were listening, answering questions, sharing with a partner, discussing with the whole class, looking at posters, watching Mrs. Brusky write her story, standing and moving, and independently writing. After each 10- to 20-minute segment of the lesson, when students' brains were ready to shift attention, Mrs. Brusky altered the activity. The students' attention did shift, but exactly to where

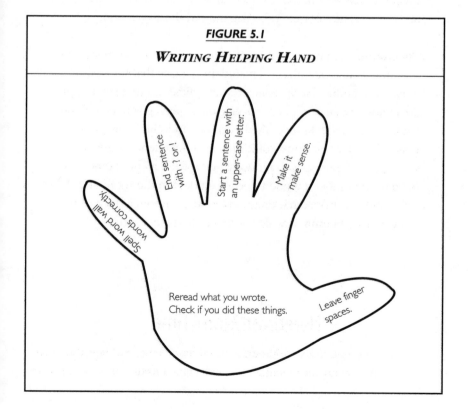

FIGURE 5.1

WRITING HELPING HAND

Spell word wall words correctly.

End sentence with . ? or !

Start a sentence with an upper-case letter.

Make it make sense.

Reread what you wrote. Check if you did these things.

Leave finger spaces.

the teacher wanted it, not to daydreaming, playing with erasers, or other behaviors not related to the lesson.

EXAMPLE: KEEPING STUDENTS ENGAGED DURING A WHOLE-CLASS DISCUSSION
ALL GRADE LEVELS

Purpose: To keep students on task by randomly calling on them during lessons.

Reasoning: Calling on only the students with their hands raised is not the best way to help all students actively listen during a discussion. You can probably recite the names of the students in your class who always have their hands raised, ready to share their thoughts, as well as the students who tend to never volunteer to answer or share. Those who rarely raise their hands to volunteer an answer may or may not have an answer in their heads, and may or may not even be listening to the discussion.

Procedures: Calling on students randomly helps to ensure that all students are listening; each student realizes that they could be held accountable for an answer at any time. Some teachers pick and choose which student to call on at any given time. Other teachers have developed methods for randomly calling on students. For example, one could have each student's name written on a tongue depressor to randomly grab from a cup. Some teachers have a number assigned to each student in the room and then pull a number from a hat or a numbered card from a deck of playing cards to determine which student will take a turn.

■ ■ ■

Need for More Time

The demands of the information era, when there is more to learn than ever before, coupled with the demands of high-stakes testing in our education system, leave teachers feeling as though they must pack more and more information into their students' brains. Unfortunately, we are given no additional time in which to accomplish this task. On the other hand, when it comes to brain-based learning, less is more. A student who is taught one or two new concepts thoroughly, over time, learns and applies the concepts more effectively than a student who is quickly exposed to 10 new concepts.

Our brains have a capacity to remember the equivalent of approximately 10 million books of 1,000 pages each. This incredible statistic would lead us to believe that remembering and learning should be an easy task. However, the rest of the story is that only one out of every hundred bits of information received by the brain makes it to long-term memory (Howard, 2000). Learning new information takes time. As we learned in Chapter 4, new information that is immediately relevant, or extremely pertinent, is typically learned quickly and easily. For example, when hired for a new job, most people remember the new boss's name immediately, and they will not forget it. In a classroom, however, much of what is learned is not transferred that quickly into long-term memory. The new concept or skill must be understood and usually related to prior knowledge or experience. The information then must be practiced or manipulated, and used or applied numerous times before it becomes ingrained in the brain's long-term memory.

Henry Holcomb, a memory researcher in Johns Hopkins University's Department of Radiology, determined that it will take five to six hours for a new motor skill memory to move from the short-term memory area in the front of the brain, where it is initially being understood and manipulated, to the long-term, permanent memory area in the back of the brain. If another new physical skill is introduced during that five- or six-hour time period, the initial learning may be hindered (Howard, 2000).

Let's suppose a student learns the new skill of dribbling a basketball. The required five to six hours is not to say he or she must practice dribbling for that amount of time before the skill is learned. Rather, after the physical practice period, up to six hours may go by before the skill of dribbling is ingrained in the brain's memory. If that student were to leave physical education class and, two hours later, learn for the first time how to jump rope at recess time, he or she may not be as adept at ball dribbling. It takes more practice and an additional five- to six-hour block of time for the brain to have another chance at thoroughly remembering how to dribble a basketball. It is recommended that if any physical activity follows learning a new motor skill, it should be one that is routine and well known.

Studies demonstrate the importance of practice and reflection for long-term memory. Adequate practice and reflection take TIME! The effects of practice on students' performance, including studies by Ross (1988), Bloom (1976), and Kumar (1991), have been synthesized in *Classroom Instruction that Works* (2001) by authors Robert Marzano, Debra Pickering, and Jane Pollock. These authors point out two significant generalizations regarding practice, both directly substantiating the need for additional time for effective learning:

1. Practice over time is necessary for mastery of a new skill. After four practice sessions, students will reach a competence level of 47.9 percent of complete mastery. It will take students 20 more practice sessions, about 24 times in all, to reach 80 percent competency.

2. Students must gain a conceptual understanding of how a new skill works. During practice sessions, students should be reflecting on the new concept and adapting or reshaping it. This deeper examination of the new concept, as well as differentiated ways of practicing through reshaping, will promote useful application of that knowledge in the future.

Robin Fogarty (1998) states that reflection is the cornerstone of intelligence-friendly classrooms.

> It drives personal application and transfer of learning. It makes learning personal, purposeful, meaningful, and relevant and gives the brain reason to pay attention, understand, and remember. Reflection is sometimes the missing piece in today's classroom puzzle, as the pacing of the school day often precludes time for reflection. Yet reflection, introspection, and mindfulness must accompany collaborations and discussions because the time for reflection is the time for internalizing the learning. (p. 657)

When teachers feel pressed for time they often cut out what are sometimes referred to as "extras" or the "fluff" in order to get in the basics. The dangerous part of this practice is that the "fluff" might actually be the learning experiences like reflection, enrichment, looking for patterns, deep discussions, sharing with peers, making projects, comparing and contrasting, or problem-solving, when the brain is manipulating and applying the new knowledge. It is these higher-level thinking processes that allow the brain to thoroughly understand the new concepts and internalize them into mean-ingful memories. It is usually far better to cut out about two-thirds of the simple, rote practice time in exchange for the more valuable synthesis, reflection, and application time of that same new knowledge. For example, if students are learning the multiplication fact of 8 × 5 = 40, do not have them waste time doing three worksheets with 20 practice problems each in which 8 × 5 shows up about every third item. Instead, have the students complete just one of those rote practice sheets and then spend the other available time genuinely working with the new concept. Have the students

- show 8 × 5 with counters,
- experiment by adding five groups of eight or eight groups of five to arrive at the product,
- compare and contrast 8 × 5 and 5 × 8,
- look for number patterns through counting by fives,
- use the 8 × 5 = 40 fact in real-life problem-solving situations.

During practice through application, the students will still see, hear, write, and feel the number fact enough times that they will likely memo-rize it while using higher-level thinking skills. For the brain's long-term memory, it is better to learn a few concepts very thoroughly than many concepts vaguely.

Organizational and Instructional Tips for Teachers

When time is limited, teachers must make every minute count for learning. The following ideas are not new or earth-shattering but simply reminders of routines that are efficient in preventing wasted time in the classroom.

- Take attendance after students have begun working on some-thing—don't waste their time with a roll call.
- As you are taking a minute to gather resources or change an over-head, have your students pair and share the most important thing they just heard you say—don't have them sit idly for that minute.
- Integrate academic subject areas—for example, don't teach subject and predicate with irrelevant sample sentences. Use sentences that pro-vide factual information about the Civil War if that is what is being stud-ied in social studies class.

- Establish the routine of having a problem of the day (a review from yesterday or a preview of what's to come today) on the board for students to work on immediately when they walk in—don't let them waste time chatting with friends as classmates trickle in and get seated.
- Offer an academic assistance program during recess at the primary level or during study hall at the secondary level.
- Use reflective practices to imbed learning into memory by using the 20-2-20 rule (described in the example below). Don't teach something once and expect mastery, but also don't practice something repeatedly in a simplistic, rote manner and expect deep understanding.

■ ■ ■

EXAMPLE: USING THE 20-2-20 RULE FOR REFLECTION
AND APPLICATION
MIDDLE AND HIGH SCHOOL LEVELS

Purpose: To improve students' application of new knowledge and skills.

Background: Ms. Balogh found that reviewing information with her middle school students and high school students the same way it had been taught the day before was not yielding deep understanding of the concepts or promoting application of the new skills. She wanted the students to have enough repetition and practice of the new concepts to learn them well enough to demonstrate using the new knowledge later in time. She began implementing the 20-2-20 rule in virtually all academic subject areas. Ms. Balogh's students were thoroughly learning the new information, could apply the concepts at a later time, and did not require time-consuming daily, rote review.

Procedures:

20 = Re-explanation within 20 minutes
Within the first 20 minutes of a lesson (around that time when students' attention is waning anyway) she has the students re-explain what they have just learned. This might take the form of a brief

class discussion, a sharing session with a partner, a drawing to show a classmate, or a written explanation in students' journals. Some form of feedback is always tied into this reflection/ re-explanation experience, sometimes from Ms. Balogh and other times from a classmate. This allows each student to know if he or she is on the right track.

2 = Review and application within two days

Within two days of the initial learning, Ms. Balogh requires her students to review and apply that new information. This often takes the form of a mind-map, a piece of writing, development of a related problem for a classmate to solve, or a brief demonstration of the newly acquired skills.

20 = Reflection and more application within 20 days

Within 20 days, usually at the end of the subject area's unit, Ms. Balogh has her students reflect on what they have learned. They apply the new concepts or skills in a more involved project, such as a debate, performance, piece of writing, or a model. These products are usually shared with the whole class or a small group within the class.

■ ■ ■

Opportune Time Periods for Learning

There is a time and place for everything. This saying is true when it comes to the brain and learning. Neuroscientists discovered long ago that particular places in the brain are responsible for different bodily functions, emotions, thinking, and learning. For example, the frontal cortex of the brain carries out deep thinking and planning, a part of the cortex called Brocas' Area allows people to speak, and the occipital lobes in the back of the brain process visual stimuli. Is it important for teachers to memorize the brain's areas and each one's functions? I don't think so. I believe that, in general, it is not crucial for teachers to know the "places" in the brain for learning. However, I do believe it is important for teachers to know the "times" in the brain for learning. Brain research provides us with three different ways to look at opportune time periods for learning:

- Within a person's lifespan.
- Within a student's day.
- Within a teacher's lesson.

Opportune Time Periods for Learning Within a Person's Lifespan

During the last two decades, scientists have found that the brain changes in response to environmental influences, particularly during prenatal and childhood periods of development. Prior to this, it was thought the brain was genetically determined, that the brain at birth is the brain for life. We also now know that during the first year of life, the brain is learning so much new information that synapses (connections between brain cells) are forming at an amazingly quick rate. A 1-year-old has as many as 1,000 trillion synapses. However, scientists also believe that after the first couple of years of life, these synapses begin an elimination process just as rapid as the original growth rate. The brain functions in a "use it or lose it" mode. If we don't keep learning and using those connections, they die. By the time a child is 10 years old, he or she has about 100 billion brain cells with 500 trillion synapses between them—the same number as an adult (Wisconsin Council on Children and Families, 1999).

Within the last two decades, positive emission tomography (PET) scans have shown that the brain has critical periods for learning during childhood. In some resources these time periods are called learning windows or windows of opportunity. I tend to veer away from those terms because we think of a window as being either open or shut. The brain is so smart and has so much potential that it is never completely shut; a person can learn new concepts and skills throughout his or her life. However, research shows there are definitely times when the window is thrown wide open for learning and development. These are the optimum times for learning in our lives, and, according to current knowledge, these times all fall within the child's first 10 years or so. According to Dr. Harry Chugani, a Wayne State University neuroscientist:

> Brain development proceeds in waves, with different parts of the brain becoming active "construction sites" at different times and with

different degrees of intensity. By studying PET scans of children . . . [he] quantified the activity levels of different parts of the brain at various stages of development. In this way, [he] gained insight into brain plasticity at particular ages. At one year of age, for example, there is intensive activity in the cortical and subcortical regions that control sensory-motor functions. . . . By about eight months, the frontal cortex shows increased metabolic activity. This part of the brain is associated with the ability to regulate and express emotion, as well as to think and to plan, and it becomes the site of frenetic activity just at the moment that babies make dramatic leaps into self-regulation and strengthen their attachment to their primary caregivers. (Wisconsin Council on Children and Families, 1999, p. 1)

Figure 5.2 represents the usual prime developmental and learning time periods (Sousa, 1998). This is not to say these are the only times these

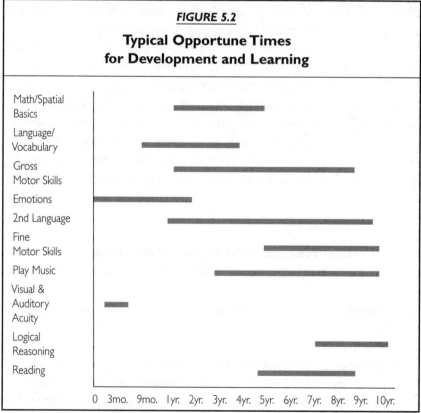

FIGURE 5.2

**Typical Opportune Times
for Development and Learning**

Adapted from *How the Brain Learns: More New Insights for Educators*, by D. Sousa, a presentation on August 18, 1998 in Port Washington, WI.

skills are developed. For example, in the area of math/spatial concepts, children are able to learn math not only from the ages of 1½ to 4½ years. These are the years when the foundation for math learning is established; at this age children will be able to understand basic math concepts like large, small, few, and many. Does this mean a person cannot learn to play an instrument, or learn new vocabulary, or learn a second language as a teenager or an adult? No, certainly not. However, it will be much more difficult beyond those optimal periods of development. Because each brain is different, some children reach these stages earlier or later, and some may progress through them more quickly and some more slowly.

It is important for parents, teachers, and school systems to be aware of these optimal learning periods for a few reasons. First, we want to hold reasonable expectations for youngsters. It is not fair for a parent or teacher of a 2-year-old child to expect him to cut on a straight line beautifully; he does not have the fine motor capabilities to complete that skill. Next, this information can make parents of young children aware of just how important those first five years are in a child's development. Also, it behooves school systems to understand that reaching out to the youngest students might prevent some learning difficulties in children as they age. And finally, it also is wise for school districts to rethink the timing of music and foreign language instruction. More often than not, these programs begin in secondary schools, when the students are well past their opportune time periods for learning those skills. Consequently, the system is setting the students up for a more difficult learning path than is necessary.

■ ■ ■

EXAMPLE: FOREIGN LANGUAGE DEVELOPMENT
BEFORE AND AFTER THE AGE OF 10

Purpose: Learning a second language is easiest before the age of 10.

Background: You probably know a few people who were not born in the United States or whose parents are from another country. Have some of these people maintained their native accent while others have not? A high school friend of mine, Sonja, speaks with no accent although both her parents speak with a strong German accent. I could never comprehend why her parents still had the accent although they had been in the country for 20 years, yet Sonja never spoke English with an accent even though she was living with and listening to her parents.

Reasoning: I now understand the reasons after reading brain research regarding language development. It's all about the magic age of 10. When a language is learned before the age of 10, the person will maintain that accent. Sonja's parents learned most of their English in their early 20s, when they moved to this country. Therefore, they have maintained their native German accent, even though they have now lived in the United States for many more years than in Germany. Sonja was born in the United States, and learned English as her primary language. Even though, as a toddler, she learned English through listening to her parents' accented language, she still had contact with enough "American-sounding" people before the age of 10 that she never developed her parents' German accent. This example is consistent with the data seen in Figure 5.2; the brain is most pliable and receptive in the area of language development before the age of 10.

■ ■ ■

Opportune Time Periods for Learning Within a Student's Day

It is early afternoon and your students are back in your classroom after lunch. You have an interesting lesson planned that you enthusiastically explain to the class, and yet they all sit there looking like slugs. What happened to those bright, motivated students you were working with during the morning? What you have in front of you are students in the downtime of the day for learning. According to studies of circadian rhythms, halfway between the time you usually wake and the time you usually go to sleep is your low point in terms of energy and alertness (Howard, 2000; Sousa, 1998). If my students wake at 6:00 a.m. and go to sleep at 9:00 p.m., around 1:00 p.m. they will be in their downtime for learning and will probably just feel like taking a nap. The scary thing is that I wake up at 5:30 a.m. and go to sleep about 10:00 p.m. which means about the time my students are ready to doze off, so am I.

The teacher has to work especially hard during that hour of downtime to keep students' brains active and alert so as not to lose an hour of learning. Hands-on lessons are better for this purpose than lectures. If possible, teachers should try to plan for this downtime by rotating instruction daily so the same academic area is not taught during this same time period. Some middle and high schools operate on a rotating schedule of classes; that is, an A day, a B day, and so on, where one class period is dropped each day on a rotating basis. While typically the main objective of this type of program is to fit in eight classes during a semester rather than just seven, a fringe benefit is not having the same course every day during students' downtime. It is conceivable that a student could end up having math instruction, for example, during the downtime of the day for several school years in a row. His or her achievement may suffer compared to that of a student with the same abilities who has math instruction during the first hour of school for several years in a row.

Teachers should also be aware that, according to research on circadian rhythms, the best time for new learning is during the first two hours after waking and during the last two hours before going to sleep (Howard, 2000). Plan the most crucial instruction during the first part of the morning and advise your students to study for tests beginning an hour or two before going to sleep for the night. Ups and downs will occur all day long in students' learning, but pay special attention to the best "up" of the day—first thing in the morning, and the worst "down" of the day—early afternoon.

■ ■ ■

EXAMPLE: COMPENSATING FOR THE DOWNTIME OF THE DAY
GRADES 9 AND 10, HISTORY

Purpose: To improve students' learning by compensating for the downtime of the day.

Background: Mr. Grieffenkamp reports that, year after year, students in his fifth period history class (in the early afternoon) do not seem to learn as much or as easily as students in the other class periods.

Procedure: He naturally began modifying lessons for those fifth period students by supplying them with improved handouts, using more visuals such as maps and pictures of people, and even having students stand up and move about the room more often, in hopes of perking them up a bit.

Results: The fifth period students did start achieving higher scores on quizzes and tests. Because it was working well with the fifth period students, Mr. Grieffenkamp began using more of these instructional strategies with his other class periods too. Soon, they too seemed to be achieving better. In fact, the students in his other classes improved to the point where the fifth period class was down to the bottom of the heap again! However, Mr. Grief-fenkamp said he didn't feel badly about that because he knew the fifth period students were learning more effectively than during his purely lecturing mode, especially during that downtime of the day.

■ ■ ■

Opportune Time Periods for Learning Within a Teacher's Lesson

In the same way that there are uptimes and downtimes for learning during the day, there are also uptimes and downtimes during each lesson. The first 10 minutes or so of a lesson are considered the time when students will learn the most (Sousa, 1998). Teachers should not use that period for review or other nonlearning tasks like taking attendance. Hit the students with the new, crucially important information right off the bat. Then, later in the lesson, tie in review from previous lessons to relate new concepts to that background knowledge.

Approximately 20 minutes into a lesson, when students' attention is naturally waning, the downtime occurs (Sousa, 1998). To accommodate this, change the delivery mode of the information for the next two to five minutes. For example, if the students had been listening to lecture, have them write a response in their journals, or, if they had been reading silently, have them turn and discuss the text with a partner.

Following this downtime in the middle of the lesson, there is a second prime time for learning. While the last 10 to 20 minutes of the lesson are not as powerful as the first 10 minutes, it is an effective learning period for the brain (Sousa, 1998). This is the time the teacher can review and relate concepts learned earlier, or have the students apply the new knowledge learned during the first prime time (Sousa, 1995).

I advise teachers of children under 3rd grade to think of their lessons in blocks of 22 minutes, even if a reading class, for example, is an hour long. Working with 3rd graders up through adult learners, think of your lesson in blocks of 44 minutes, even if you are presenting to these people all day long. This will automatically assist you in adjusting for the attention span of your class. See Figure 5.3.

■ ■ ■

EXAMPLE: TAKING ATTENDANCE DURING NONINSTRUCTIONAL TIMES HIGH SCHOOL AND GRADE 5

Purpose: To maximize the use of the most opportune learning period during lessons by altering attendance-taking procedures.

Sample 1: One chemistry teacher does not want to use any of the prime time for learning to take attendance. Rather than taking a roll call, he starts right into the instruction for the day. Usually after 5 to 10 minutes of an explanation, he has the students get started working in the lab section of the classroom. Only when they are all working and learning does he glance around the room, noting who is absent and remembering if anyone was tardy. The high school's attendance secretary copes with the fact the teacher's attendance slip is simply 10 minutes later than most of the other classrooms' slips, especially after he explained his reasoning to her.

Sample 2: Ms. Hartzell, a 5th grade teacher, also does not want to waste valuable instruction time taking attendance or doing the hot

FIGURE 5.3

Planning Lessons Using Short Blocks of Time

1st Grade Reading	6th Grade Math	High School Earth Science	Adults' Brain Seminar
1st Prime Time 10 minutes: Teacher reads aloud a new book to the class, having students make predictions and look at the pictures.	**1st Prime Time 20 minutes:** Teacher explains the new concept of equivalent fractions by using visuals/manipulatives at the front of the room while students use the same at their desks.	**1st Prime Time 20 minutes:** Teacher explains and draws on the chalkboard the new concept of kettle lake formation. Students take notes.	**1st Prime Time 20 minutes:** Presenter tells, and shows using overheads or Powerpoint, the top five latest and greatest brain-based learning tips for teachers.
Downtime 2 minutes: Students turn to a partner to tell their favorite part of the story.	**Downtime 4 minutes:** Students walk to a new area of the room to work with a partner, quizzing each other on equivalent fractions.	**Downtime 4 minutes:** Brief portion of a video or pictures are shown of kettle lakes and surrounding areas.	**Downtime 4 minutes:** Participants write a reaction to or practical application of the information just heard.
2nd Prime Time 10 minutes: Teacher writes new vocabulary words from the book on the chalkboard, discussing initial sounds and spelling patterns.	**2nd Prime Time 20 minutes:** Students work independently to develop several of their own problems and an answer key. These problems are sent home with a partner as a portion of the night's math homework.	**2nd Prime Time 20 minutes:** Teacher prefaces a reading assignment by relating previously learned information to the new information about the formation of kettle lakes. The students are grouped in triads. Each member has five minutes to explain the formation of one glacial feature: doldrums, glacially scoured lakes, or kettle lakes.	**2nd Prime Time 20 minutes:** Participants stand and move to a new area of the room to form small groups. The groups discuss application ideas for use in classrooms regarding the latest brain information.

(continued)

FIGURE 5.3 (continued)

Planning Lessons Using Short Blocks of Time

1st Grade Reading	6th Grade Math	High School Earth Science	Adults Brain Seminar
Brief Break: Stand, get a drink of water.	**Brief Break:** Students gather or put away math materials and prepare for next subject area or class.	**Brief Break:** A reading assignment is given for homework. Students gather materials and leave for their next class.	**Brief Break:** Participants walk back to original seats, probably grabbing a coffee or donut refill on the way.
1st Prime Time 10 minutes: Students now read their own copy of the same story.			**Remainder of the Seminar:** The day is broken into 44-minute periods of varying information and activities, with breaks provided in between.
Downtime 2 minutes: Students write a sentence about a character in the story.			
2nd Prime Time 10 minutes: Students draw a picture of a different ending to the story that could have been used.			

lunch count. She uses a speedy system wherein each student, as they walk through the classroom doorway, moves a Velcro-covered bingo chip away from his or her name and places it either in the hot lunch or cold lunch column on the name/attendance chart. When the tardy bell rings, students are in their seats, ready to learn, and the attendance and lunch count are already done. With a quick glance at the chart, Ms. Hartzell can see how many students are buying hot lunch and take attendance by recording those students with a chip remaining next to their names.

■ ■ ■

Time Is on Your Side

Armed with information from brain research regarding time and learning, time can be on the side of teachers. Teachers may never feel that they have enough time, but the following ideas can help teachers use their time with students in a way that optimizes learning:

• Realize that, in terms of curriculum to cover, less is more; delving deeper into a few topics creates more meaningful, long-lasting knowledge than skimming over many topics.

• Integrate or combine academic areas to kill two birds with one stone, thus sparing precious instructional time.

• Reconsider time-on-task expectations to help students.

• Understand and adhere to optimum learning times in a lifetime to make learning easier for students.

• Implement instructional practices exercising prime time and downtime principles, during every lesson, every day, to maximize learning.

In a nutshell, make every minute count!

Implementing Relevant Brain-Compatible Ideas

Time on Task
- Expect students to pay attention to one form of instruction for no more than 20 minutes.
- Control students' attention shifts with a new teaching method before their attentions shifts without you.
- Make learning interesting and fun so students want to stay on task.
- Keep all students engaged by calling on them all randomly, not just those with hands raised.

Need for More Time
- Use review through application regularly. Some concepts take 24 repetitions before mastery.
- Incorporate time for reflection into everyday classroom practices. It allows students' brains to develop meaning and personal relevance from the concepts introduced by the teacher.
- Integrate one subject's concepts into other academic areas. It makes sense to the brain and frees up time for high-level thinking and thorough application of the skills in lessons.
- Use the 20-2-20 rule: Re-explain within 20 minutes, review and apply within 2 days, reflect upon and further apply within 20 days.
- Make every minute count toward learning!

Opportune Time Periods for Learning Within a Person's Lifespan
- Share opportune ages for particular learning and development with parents. They are the primary teachers for their children, at least during the first five years of life.
- Don't consider music, art, drama, physical education, and second languages as "fluff" in elementary school curriculum. Delaying instruction in these areas until secondary school makes mastery more difficult for the students.
- Don't expect logical, adultlike thinking and understanding from students who are too young for it.

Opportune Time Periods for Learning Within a Student's Day
- Arrange the classroom schedule with circadian rhythms in mind; maximize the use of the brain's most alert times.
- Teach the most important lesson first thing in the morning.
- Incorporate very active learning during the downtime of the day (early afternoon) to keep the brain and body engaged in learning.
- Rotate students' daily instructional schedules so the same class is not always taught during the downtime of the day.

Opportune Time Periods for Learning Within a Teacher's Lesson
- Think of lessons in 22- or 44-minute blocks of time, depending on the learner's age.
- Use the first 10–20 minutes (1st prime time) of each lesson for teaching the new, most important information. Do not use that time for review or noninstructional tasks.
- Alter the mode of learning during the two–four minutes of downtime in the middle of the lesson.
- Use the last 10–20 minutes (2nd prime time) of each lesson for tying the new information to past learning or for application of the new concepts.

6

Enrichment for the Brain

PICTURE A KOOSH BALL IN YOUR MIND. WE WANT OUR STUDENTS' BILLIONS OF brain cells to be as full and bushy as Koosh Balls, with hundreds of dendrites reaching out for new connections. It is through these connections that the human brain grows in knowledge and skills. And it is through many forms of enrichment that the teacher can foster rapid dendrite growth with minimal effort or direct instruction. You will learn from examples in this chapter that daily enrichment for your students' brains can be as easy as asking the right questions, pushing a button on a compact disk player, designing a bulletin board, putting out some puzzles, or using colors to show patterns. Examples of classroom enrichment for the brain fall into three key categories:
- Problem solving.
- Music.
- Physical environment.

Enrichment for the Brain Through Problem Solving

As the scientific, medical, and educational fields' specialists are discovering volumes of new information about the human brain and how it learns, many different recommendations of brain-based learning strategies are being conveyed to teachers. Of the dozens of ideas and strategies, one that would appear to be the most universally accepted as highly effective in enriching the brain is problem solving. In fact, Eric Jensen (1998) asserts that challenging problem solving is the single best way to enrich the brain.

97

This type of problem solving is not of the 2 + 2 = 4 variety, where there is one correct answer. Rather, it is the problem solving that involves reasoning, critical thinking, and other high-level thinking skills. Problem solving is the most beneficial when it involves various sections of the brain at the same time; multiple neural pathways are developed in students' minds when we facilitate problem solving by pairing a class discussion with building a model, sketching a picture, or watching a demonstration. Plus, the nifty thing about problem solving is that the brain really doesn't care if it ever discovers a solution or not; it is the high-level thinking process that develops new dendrites in the brain, making it grow more intelligent (Sylwester, 1995).

The easiest part for the teacher about facilitating problem solving is the fact that the students should do the work, not the teacher. Conversely, the hardest thing about facilitating problem solving is the fact that the students should do the work, not the teacher. Beginning a problem-solving lesson, or impromptu high-level thinking session, may be as simple as asking a question. As the adult who knows one solution, it may be difficult not to jump in and give an answer . . . don't do it! Your answer may not be what they are striving for anyway. The students must make their own way through the problem-solving process to reap the benefits of brainstorming, reasoning, trial and error, critical thinking, contemplating cause and effect, and drawing conclusions. Problem solving is discovery learning at its finest. The most a teacher should do is to guide students through some possible steps in the thinking processes, to be a cheerleader along the way so they don't give up when frustration sets in, and sometimes, in the end, to convince them there may not be one correct solution to a problem.

■ ■ ■

EXAMPLE: PROBLEM SOLVING WITH GLOBAL ISSUES
GRADE 3 THROUGH HIGH SCHOOL

Purpose: To teach students to see both the pros and cons of a situation and to brainstorm potential solutions to a problem.

Background: Teaching students to become productive members of society is typically a part of any school district's mission statement. Our education system must produce good problem solvers because, the fact is, our world has a lot of problems that need to be solved. Whether they are dealing with massive issues like global warming or religious warfare or seemingly insignificant questions like whether to widen a local street to a four-lane highway, we hope our youth will be prepared to not only cope with problems but solve them as well.

Lesson: The following 3rd grade example could easily be modified to fit older students' maturity levels, background knowledge, and research skills.

During a social studies unit, a class learned that the earth's rainforests are being cut down at the rate of one football-field-size parcel of land every minute. The class brainstormed reasons for this occurrence and the resulting negative consequences. They quickly saw rainforest destruction as a huge problem. The teacher asked the students what could be done to end rainforest destruction.

That question led to three class periods worth of discussion, research, statistics being put into graphs, and, on the third day, a class debate. The teacher led an organized debate because, as the students learned the reasoning behind cutting down rainforest trees, slash-and-burn farming, and harvesting plants for medicinal purposes, some students saw positive outcomes and others expressed only negative feelings toward the results. Curbing the arguments brewing between students, they were assigned to be either a "pro" participant or a "con" participant and had to defend that side of each issue raised. Some students had an easy time vehemently defending their side because they truly believed in it. Others had to stretch their minds to understand and defend a viewpoint they believed to be invalid. In the end of this particular debate, the class came to a consensus that rainforest destruction is generally a bad thing.

They finally moved into some problem solving regarding how to curb the current destruction. They listed their potential solutions, wrote a letter to their local state senator about laws that they believed should be imposed in our country to curtail rainforest destruction and (to some adults' chagrin) asked their parents to sign a statement saying they would no longer buy furniture of teak or mahogany wood that was cut from a rainforest.

Results: Will one 3rd grade class's efforts radically slow global warming due to rainforest destruction? No. Will one of those students continue their passion for the topic, possibly growing up to become a world leader of one kind or another who could change laws? It is always a possibility.

EXAMPLE: PROBLEM SOLVING WITH CURRENT EVENTS
ANY GRADE LEVEL

Purpose: To familiarize students with current events and their corresponding problems and potential solutions.

Lesson: Following the terrorist attacks on New York City and Washington, D.C., on September 11, 2001, a high school social studies class held a discussion about the suspected perpetrators of the attacks before their regular class began. The teacher heard strong words coming from the students about getting back at Afghanistan as a country. The teacher took the opportunity to have them read newspaper articles about that country and its people.

During the class period, they learned that many of the citizens of Afghanistan felt victimized by Osama Bin Laden and the Taliban regime. They learned about the hunger and drought that has affected the people of Afghanistan for years. They learned about a country whose people were not allowed to listen to music and world news on radios and where women were to essentially stay in their homes with painted-over windows.

The problem raised by the teacher was, "How do we retaliate against the Taliban without further devastating the citizens of Afghanistan?" The class brainstormed and discussed some options. Less than a month later, when the United States began retaliation efforts against the Taliban's strategic sites and military training centers in Afghanistan, the students understood why the United States chose the particular locations to strike with missiles. The students were also pleased to learn that food and medical supplies were dropped by planes for the citizens of Afghanistan because that actually had been one of their ideas raised during class discussions.

EXAMPLE: PROBLEM SOLVING OUTSIDE OF DAILY INSTRUCTION
GRADE 7

Purpose: To practice problem solving and other high-level thinking skills through a gamelike activity.

Background: One 7th grade teacher used specific problem-solving exercises during extra class time. The kids enjoyed the brain-teasers so much that this practice became a reward they would ask for and work toward.

Procedures: The teacher would say one sentence that would essentially be the ending or summary of a story that the class would have to backtrack and problem-solve to uncover. They could ask the teacher (who knew the whole story) only yes and no questions. So, for example, one story ending was, "The person who drank quickly lived and the person who drank slowly died." After many minutes of questioning, the 7th graders were able to ascertain, through the yes and no answers provided by the teacher, that the scenario was that two people each ordered the same drink in a restaurant. They both had poison in the ice cubes. The one who drank it slowly died because the ice had time to melt, allowing the poison to be consumed by the drinker.

The toughest problem to solve for that class had been, "If he had seen the sawdust, he wouldn't have died." It took a few Friday afternoons to figure out all the details of that, with many of the students' families at home being driven crazy wondering what exactly the scenario could be; several parents sent yes and no questions back to the teacher with their 7th graders. Does this make you curious as to what the story is about? You can e-mail me to find out.

EXAMPLE: PROBLEM SOLVING AND PROVOKING
HIGHER-LEVEL THINKING
ANY GRADE LEVEL

Purpose: To promote high-level thinking skills in students through the use of complex questions.

Reasoning: The most effective way to foster effective problem solving in students is to infuse this and other higher-level thinking skills into everyday practices. One way to do this is to ask thought-provoking questions of our students at school and encourage parents to use them at home.

Samples:

- When you think about _____, what are some of the things you wonder about?
- If you were going to solve _____ again, what would you do differently?
- What are some other ways you could get the same result?
- How do you think _____ and _____ are related?
- How is this similar to a different type of problem?
- _____ is the answer. Make up a tough question regarding it.
- Give two reasons why _____ can't be the correct answer.
- Explain three steps that you took in your thinking to arrive at your solution.
- If telling a friend about this situation, how would you summarize it?
- Compare and contrast _____ and _____.
- When you get older, how do you think your opinion might change on that?
- Which is better and why?
- Would you rather _____ or _____? Why?
- Would _____ happen like this on any other day?
- Why? Why? Why?

■ ■ ■

Enrichment for the Brain Through Music

A B C D E F G—is it hard for you to recite the alphabet without the letters coming out in a sing-songy manner? We all know how we learned the alphabet! Experientially, we know there is something special about music. It can help us remember things, like a sequence of 26 unrelated symbols known as our alphabet. It can reflect and affect our moods and our activity rate. It seems easy to remember the words of a song that we haven't heard in years, yet if those words were not put to music, we most likely couldn't correctly remember them. Over the last decade or two, research has been done to support the idea that music does have an effect on the brain. This brain research has provided us with some of the answers to some of the questions, with surely more to come during the next decade or two. Research shows that music can be used by the brain for **arousal**, as a **carrier**, or as a **primer** (Sousa, 1995).

Music for Brain Arousal

Music clearly affects people's emotions and moods. Without the eerie background music, a horror movie is not all that scary. Listening to "Gonna Fly Now" (the theme from *Rocky*) makes you feel pumped up, while other songs may bring tears to your eyes. Arousal means that the music either increases or decreases the amount of neurotransmitters, like endorphins, cortisol, and epinephrine, which are chemicals involved in the link between emotions and memories. Scientists have used PET scans to watch particular areas of the brain involved with emotions increase activity as different pieces of music are played (Wolfe, 2001). In studying the effect of music on the moods and physical condition of the body, Glenn Wilson found that

• Repetitive rhythms, such as Ravel's "Bolero" and the minimalist music of Philip Glass, induce a trancelike state that occasionally borders on ecstasy.

• Musical rhythms liberate the mind from ordinary states—hence the popularity of music in religious and military settings.

• Music that slows gradually has a gradually relaxing effect.

• Lullabies in many cultures imitate the breathing rhythms that occur in sleep.

- The body's rhythms will adapt to the rhythms of live, close-by music.
- In all cultures, observers are able to correctly identify the music of other cultures that is intended to covey specific human moods and needs, such as war, mourning, love, hunting, and sleep inducement (that is, lullabies) (Howard, 2000).

■ ■ ■

EXAMPLE: USE OF MUSIC IN SCHOOL FOR BRAIN AROUSAL PURPOSES (CALMING DURING TEST TAKING AND BUILDING EXCITEMENT FOR LESSONS) ANY GRADE LEVEL

Purpose: To effectively use music to calm students.

Background: As a teacher, I was always looking for ways to improve testing situations for my students. I had heard that playing calming background music was good for testing situations. After doing some reading, I learned that playing Baroque music, which are nonlyrical tunes of 60 beats per minute, is supposed to relax the heartbeat down to that rate and clear the mind for concentration.

Procedures: I purchased a couple of Gary Lamb's CDs (Golden Gate Records, 1992) to try out in my classroom. My students seemed to get the most uptight over math tests, so I quietly played the Baroque music in the background. The first time I tried it, I explained to the students my reason for playing it and the research I had discovered. I read them the information right from the CD packaging that professes this music will "enhance learning in children of all ages. . . . Play this music in the classroom and at home to increase intelligence and to improve productivity and concentration during testing and silent reading." I figured that even if the music had no effect itself, just using the theory of mind over matter and telling the students the music would help their intelligence couldn't hurt.

Results: I did not carry out a genuine experiment to determine if the music had an effect on test scores. However, I did definitely notice students were more relaxed when taking the test. When I would forget to start the background music during a math test, a student (usually Abby) would quickly remind me to turn it on. At the very least, I believe that they believed it helped them. A side note—the use of calming, Baroque background music might be useful for teachers to try during "hot" parent meetings. Now, as a principal, I am going to try it!

Purpose: To effectively use music to excite students.

Background: Sometimes during instruction, teachers want the opposite effect of the calmness induced by Baroque music; they want to perk up, rejuvenate, inspire those students! Use music to do it.

Examples:
- A high school teacher plays the theme from *Mission Impossible* by Lalo Schifen, challenging students to conquer a tough calculus brainteaser on the chalkboard.
- A middle school teacher blares "Takin' Care of Business" by Bachman-Turner Overdrive as students clean up litter in the schoolyard on Earth Day.
- An elementary teacher plays "Nutcracker Suite" by Tchaikovsky prior to the students beginning the reading of the children's trade book *The Nutcracker Ballet* by Deborah Hautzig.
- An elementary school (as described in Chapter 2) blares the theme from *Rocky* as students and staff enter an all-school, end-of-the-quarter Celebration Assembly.
- A preschool teacher sings a catchy clean-up tune to cue students that it is time to sing along and clean up their toys.

■ ■ ■

Music as a Carrier

As a carrier, the melody of the music acts as the vehicle for the words themselves in a way that dramatically helps memory and recall. Think about how many words are in a typical song you hear on the radio. Think of one of your favorite songs. Can you remember all those words to recite them or write them down? Probably not. But when that song comes on the radio you can probably sing along from start to finish.

From the time we are very young, we remember more easily that which is put to music or rhyme. It is hard to imagine a 3-year-old child, for example, being able to memorize dozens of pages of prose writing no matter how many time we read it to him or her. However, when put in the form of songs or nursery rhymes, children can remember quite a lot. At the beginning of this chapter, learning the alphabet was mentioned. Memorizing 26 unrelated bits of information is really quite a feat, especially considering the fact that the brain is most efficient at remembering strings of seven items or fewer. Remembering a phone number of 7 numbers, or even 10 numbers with the area code, can give some of us trouble initially but is usually manageable. Would it be hard for you to memorize a phone number that is 26 numbers long? Sure seems like it would be—but if put to music like the 26 alphabet letters have been, maybe it wouldn't be so hard after all.

■ ■ ■

EXAMPLE: MUSIC AS A MEMORY DEVICE
KINDERGARTEN, GRADE 4, AND GRADE 11,
RECENT HISTORY

Purpose: To improve students' long-term memory and recall through the use of music.

Sample 1: A kindergarten teacher, according to the prescribed curriculum, was to teach the students' phone numbers to those children who didn't already know them. In the lesson, the teacher set up five stations for each child to visit while carrying their own phone number written on an index card.

Station 1: Students each write their name and phone number in at least four friends' homemade phone books.

Station 2: Students recite their phone number while stepping on the numbers that were drawn out on a large, homemade paper phone on the floor.

Station 3: Students write their phone number in shaving cream spread around on a table.

Station 4: Students pick out, from a pile of number flashcards, the seven numbers in their own phone number and arrange them in correct order.

Station 5: Students learn and sing a quick, rhyming song that the teacher makes up for each student's phone number. For example, "555-3675, that's my phone number, no jive."

This entire lesson was very brain compatible in that the students were experiencing, moving, learning within different learning styles and multiple intelligences, working with peers, and so on. While each station certainly helped the students memorize their phone numbers, it was the little rhyming song that the students were singing or humming the rest of the day!

Sample 2: A 4th grade teacher was frustrated that many of her students did not have their multiplication facts memorized although it had been part of the previous year's curriculum. She did not want to spend weeks of class time having the students work on memorizing them, yet she found assigning flashcard practice for homework was not yielding the results she had hoped for either. She purchased a commercial tape of a "Multiplication Rap." The students had fun listening to it and were picking up on its tune and the lyrics quickly, thus learning their multiplication facts. One group of "too-cool" boys didn't like the tape, so they were charged with writing their own song or rap that was better. They did so, mainly on their own time, and had those facts memorized really quickly!

Sample 3: Roger Taylor, an educational consultant, describes one high school teacher's use of the song "We Didn't Start the Fire" by Billy Joel in his recent history class. This song contains many stanzas of quickly sung events, names, places, and phrases, each describing a decade of history during the '50s, '60s, '70s, and '80s. The high school teacher essentially used this song to outline the historical topics the class would study. The students heard the song played frequently and many of the events, people, and places mentioned in the song were studied during the semester. The semester exam simply consisted of the lyrics to "We Didn't Start the Fire" written out for each student. They were to pick a particular number of historical people, places, or events from each stanza to write about, allowing the teacher to assess their knowledge. My guess is that, in future years, whenever that song was heard by those students, it provided them with a built-in review of all that recent history they had learned in the class.

■ ■ ■

Music as a Primer

The vast majority of research involving music and the brain has been in the area of music as a primer, priming or preparing the brain's neural pathways for learning other information. Research findings support a high correlation between pitch discrimination and reading skills, and between playing the piano and mathematical/spatial/reasoning abilities (Sousa, 1995). Even popular press, during the decade of the '90s, has highlighted the effect of music on intelligence within brain-related articles: "Music . . . trains the brain for higher forms of thinking" (Begley, 1996). The danger with popular press covering medical research is that one person reads the article and discusses it with a friend, who tells another friend about it, who tells a neighbor about the information, and pretty soon we have people telling others that playing classical music to a baby will yield genius-level intelligence as an adult. The "Mozart Effect" is a term known by many, but not many know what studies were carried out and what the results actually showed (Wolfe, 2001).

Have you ever wondered why Mozart's music seems to have greater significance to the brain over other classical composers' music? Frances Rauscher and her colleagues believe that Mozart's music in particular affects the brain because of this composer's uniqueness in the following characteristics (Howard, 2000):

1. Everyone seems to like his music.

2. Of all his compositions, there are no losers; they all seem to be masterpieces.

3. Mozart began composing at only 4 or 5 years old, which is close to the age when the brain's opportune time period for learning music is just beginning.

These researchers hypothesize that Mozart's own brain was probably perfectly suited to musical composition. It is thought that his pieces are near perfection and, therefore, are well suited for other brains as well (Howard, 2000). It may be of significance, or at least interest, that the alphabet song is also the tune of "Twinkle, Twinkle Little Star." This music was composed by Mozart. Maybe Mozart's child-aged brain composed a piece that is ideal for other child-aged brains to learn and readily remember.

Enrichment for the Brain Through the Physical Environment

An elementary school teacher, a middle school teacher, and a high school teacher are sitting around a table at their district's central office waiting for a meeting to begin. The elementary teacher groans, "Another month has gone by. I really need to change all my bulletin boards." To which the middle school teacher mutters, "You mean we're supposed to *change* the bulletin boards?!" And the high school teacher simply quizzically says, "Bulletin boards? What bulletin boards?"

Admittedly, this is a very stereotypical joke that is likely unfair to many middle and high school teachers. It does, however, point out that students' surroundings are important and do need attention from teachers. Some statistics tell us that over half of what a student learns does not come from what the teacher is saying but rather from the surrounding environment (Jensen, 1998). Therefore, teachers need to make their physical classrooms true learning environments. As the students' minds and eyes wander during the day, do you want them looking at the same poster week after week, month after month? Or, worse yet, do you want them looking at a blank wall? Teachers can create classrooms that are aesthetically pleasing and comfortable while at the same time educational and functional. Some brain-compatible decorating ideas:

- Pin up posters of positive affirmations and change them weekly.
- Exhibit students' work to promote a sense of pride.
- Be sure your classroom rules or expectations are posted.
- Display useful items to students like your grading scale, calendar of events, lunch menu, classroom job chart, and so on.
- Use the ceilings to show off student work or even posters of helpful tips. It would be great for a student who was lazy and off-task, rolling his head back to stare at the ceiling tiles. Instead of seeing the blank ceiling, he would see a poster that says, "Practice makes perfect" or "Attitude is a little thing that makes a big difference."
- For pre- and early reading grade levels, label items around the classroom with words—*door, math center, word wall, clock,* and so on. Students will learn to read these words without instruction.
- Give each student the chance to design and paint his or her own cinderblock or 10" x 10" space on the wall.
- Have a few giant pillows or beanbag chairs available for comfortable reading.
- Provide a homey touch with a lamp and houseplants. (Remember from Chapter 3 that the oxygen given off by these plants is good for the brain too.)

Another way schools can increase the classroom environment's brain compatibility is to budget for the replacement of chalkboards with whiteboards in order to use more color when teaching. If the budget doesn't allow for whiteboards, teachers could use colored chalk. Whether writing on whiteboards or overhead transparencies, or even using colored chalk, stressing key points in color can boost memory retention by up to 25 percent (Jensen, 1998). When using color, teachers should follow a logical sequence because the brain is pattern seeking. Have students try using colored pens for some of their note taking to see if it helps their recall of information on tests.

Even the smell of a classroom can affect the brain and learning. Fresh air is always better than stuffy, stale air, so try to open windows whenever possible. Other scents, such as peppermint, lavender, lemon, jasmine, and lily of the valley, have been shown to improve performance and increase alertness and productivity (Howard, 2000). I believe teachers need to use common sense when using scents in classrooms. Dousing a classroom with jasmine air freshener, for example, could be very bothersome to someone sensitive to smells. However, it might be interesting to try a hint of any of the recommended scents, especially during the "downtime" after lunch, to see if students will indeed seem more alert. Research also suggests that smells might affect the limbic system in the brain, which controls some of the emotional and memory operations. This means smells can generate memories and strong emotional responses. Many of us have seen this principle in action when people reminisce over smells. Both positive and negative memories can be triggered from the smell of something burning, colognes, baby powder, a particular person's odor, and so on. A related interesting experiment to try in a classroom would be to teach a topic with the scent of, let's say, cinnamon in the room. Later, during a test on that same topic, have cinnamon in the room to see if it stimulates stronger recall. People can remember information by returning to the spot they heard it—can they remember information by smelling scents that were present when they learned it?

Lifelong Enrichment

"Use it or lose it" is the manner in which the human brain operates; if brain cells are not sparked to grow new dendrites through learning, they will die. That is why babies are born with trillions of brain cells, yet adults have only a couple hundred billion left. Sadly, trained educators typically have very little influence over children from infancy through 5 years old, when those trillions of brain cells are especially hungry for growth. However, it is never too late to grow new dendrites by learning new information and skills. Even the very elderly are advised by experts to keep their minds enriched through reading, crossword puzzles, and meeting new people. Teachers have an awesome and exciting responsibility for changing students' lives by helping them to learn. Any little thing a teacher can do, from changing instructional bulletin boards frequently to playing Baroque music during tests, just might help students learn a little bit more and achieve a little bit better. Teaching problem-solving strategies and teaching through the use of problem solving is arguably the best way to enrich the brain, to grow new dendrites, and to add knowledge and skills to students' repertoire. Grow those Koosh Ball-like dendrites in your students' brains!

Implementing Relevant Brain-Compatible Ideas:

Enrichment Through Problem Solving
- Place puzzles or brainteasers around the classroom for students to use during idle minutes of free time.
- Implement a problem of the day.
- When asking questions, never accept just a yes or no answer. Always ask the follow-up of "why" or "how."
- Don't give students all the information. Allow their brains to contemplate information and draw conclusions.
- Involve high-level thinking in every lesson, every day. Simply asking the right questions can do this.

Enrichment Through Music
- Use uplifting songs to spark enthusiasm and energy.
- Play Baroque music in the background to promote a calming, thinking environment.
- When students are having trouble memorizing information, have them create a song to help remember the information.
- Try commercial music CDs that exist on a wide range of educational topics from multiplication facts to the Constitution.
- Inform parents of the benefits of learning to play a musical instrument between the ages of 3 and 10.

Enrichment Through the Physical Environment
- Allow students to make the classroom their own; permit each student to bring a favorite item like a poster, memento, or trinket to exhibit.
- Change bulletin boards frequently—at least once per month—so students are able to learn new information from them.
- Display useful information to students in the classroom (lunch menu, classroom rules, grading scale, etc.).
- Use patterns of colors during instruction to increase memory.
- Try the use of productivity-enhancing scents in the classroom.
- Bring in a lamp and houseplants to foster a homey feeling in the classroom.
- Keep lighting bright enough. Even when showing a video or overhead transparencies, never turn off all the lights.

7

Assessment and Feedback

THE MAIN LEARNING GOALS ARE TO UNDERSTAND THE CONCEPTS WELL, TO REMEM-
ber them always, and to use them readily. How do we know when a student has reached this level of learning, or mastery, of the concepts? We
learn this through worthwhile assessment. The main assessment goals are
to determine what students have learned, to ensure they can apply the
new knowledge, and to guide teachers in planning future instruction.

Assessment exists in both formal and informal methods. Both of these
methods give valuable yet very different information to either the teacher,
the student, or, ideally, both. Assessment can range from a nationally
norm-referenced, standardized test to a peer examining another student's
project. The results or feedback received from any form of assessment and
what is done with the results are the crucial elements in making assessment meaningful. Feedback can range from a percentile score on a norm-
referenced test to a comment like, "Hey, that's really good" from one student to another. Assessment and feedback are integral parts of the
learning process, not the end of the learning event.

Assessment

New understandings about the brain and learning necessitate a fresh look
at assessment practices being used in our schools. Successful learning was
once viewed as accurate memorization; the more facts a student could
spew out, the smarter he or she must be. Educators now realize we live in
an information-rich society. A student can obtain virtually any information
that is needed by double-clicking on an Internet icon. It is the acquisition

and application of useful knowledge and skills, rather than memorization of facts, that defines a true act of learning. In other words, it is what the student can do with information that really determines the level of understanding and achievement. Facts alone constitute very little knowledge without deeper understanding of their meaning and how we use them. Real learning is much more than regurgitating the beginning dates of wars and their battles, for example. Real learning is applying knowledge and skills in contextual situations and solving real-life problems with new, creative solutions (Ronis, 2000). For example, students can compare those initial dates of wars to the economic conditions at the time in order to identify patterns. Then, applying their conclusions to current times, they can determine if there are related ways to predict or even prevent future wars. Learning to remember trivia may prepare students to be successful on a TV game show such as "Who Wants to Be a Millionaire." Learning to apply the trivia or knowledge, along with skills of high-level thinking and problem solving, prepares the student to be successful in life.

As the paradigm shifts in education toward teaching more meaningful concepts and skills, assessment practices must change as well. In-depth evaluation of learning means setting aside those number two pencils, because Scantron tests alone will not do the trick. Assessment must be an ongoing part of the learning process and, as often as possible, should be as authentic as the learning. For example, if a student is supposed to have learned how to recognize a chemical reaction, do not assess learning with a multiple-choice test item. Instead, have the student recreate a chemical reaction that has been practiced in class. The student can then show and describe the reaction, maybe comparing and contrasting it with two other chemicals that do not react. Teachers must also keep in mind, when planning assessments, that each child is unique. Classroom assessment should not always mean a test and should not always be the same for each student.

Standardized Tests

Richard Stiggins (1994) asserts in his second principle of sound assessment that "classroom assessments exert greatest influence on student learning and academic self-concept." Although standardized local, state, and national testing hit the newspapers, the daily forms of classroom assessments provide the most meaningful information to the teacher and, more importantly, to the students. Classroom assessment is closely aligned to instruction and therefore reveals more significant data for determining what a student has learned and for driving instruction than any test imposed from outside the classroom (Stiggins, 1994).

The use of standardized tests began in the early years of the 20th century in response to the scientific testing movement—at a time when the American public, educators, and politicians felt the need for objective measurements for comparison purposes. Mass-produced tests could be given to large numbers of students with distinct, numerical scores that were easy to report (Ronis, 2000). The problem occurs when this form of testing is perceived as the complete picture of what a student has learned. More accurately, it is a one-day glance at what a student may know, through primarily foundation-level, multiple-choice questions that may or may not correspond with the curriculum covered by that point during the school year. Standardized tests tend to reveal what information students have or have not memorized rather than how well they can apply knowledge, think through situations, problem-solve, compare and contrast, draw conclusions, create models, and so on. Standardized tests do show how students compare to other students, but they tell almost nothing about an individual's learning and progress. Only alternative assessments reveal the more meaningful information—information that shows where a student stands in relation to specific learning goals for the instruction and learning occurring in the classroom.

However, I also believe that standardized tests can serve a useful purpose in an education system. While they are not the most reliable assessment for evaluating an individual student's knowledge or achievement, they can expose more global generalizations regarding instructional patterns in a school or school district. Most standardized testing companies offer students' test results in a variety of formats that may be purchased and sent back to the school. Rather than only receiving the students' individual profile sheets, which are typically sent home to parents as well as filed in cumulative folders, it is worth the extra cost to purchase the testing data by subject area objectives and items. It is analysis of these data that reveals instructional strengths and weaknesses over time. When faculty members can see, for example, that a higher percentage of students are performing poorly on "number sense" on the math subtest than any other math objective, they may realize that it is time to improve instruction in that area.

However, drawing conclusions from standardized tests must be done carefully by looking at data from different perspectives and over multiple years. Last year at my school a large number of 4th graders missed the same three test items on editing skills in the language arts subtest. It could have been easy to jump to the conclusion that instruction at our school must be weak in editing skills. However, after looking more closely at the test, we found that those three items happened to be the last three items in the language arts portion of the test. As it turned out, our students were simply running out of time. Did we change instructional practices in how editing skills were being taught? No, that wasn't warranted. What we did discuss at a faculty meeting was the practice of warning students a few minutes before the testing time is up to help them budget their time. Some teachers also thought it might be helpful to familiarize students with time limits during language arts lessons and, therefore, began implementing periodic timed exercises with their students. These teachers believe that students were used to time pressures in math with timed facts quizzes, but were rarely exposed to time pressures in other academic areas. Yes, standardized assessments can provide us with trends and general conclusions about some instructional practices and testing format needs. But to discover what a student truly knows, understands, and can apply, alternative classroom assessments are the key.

Alternative Assessments

Teachers must keep in mind that assessments and tests are not necessarily the same things. Tests are just one form of assessment. Alternative assessments are all forms of assessment other than standardized tests (Ronis, 2000). Alternative assessments are student centered and curriculum based, and, therefore, far more brain compatible than standardized tests. These assessments may be formal, with the teacher diligently recording scores, data, information, and observations, and providing specific and organized feedback for the student. Or alternative assessments may be informal. During informal assessments the teacher usually makes frequent, spontaneous observations or holds conversations with more impromptu feedback given to the student. The main difference between formal and informal alternative assessments is the level and amount of planning. Informal assessments are not necessarily less valuable for the teacher or the student than formal assessment practices. Both can yield important information for the student and the teacher about what has been learned and what still needs to be learned. Brain-compatible instruction is based on active learning and emotional engagement, consideration of students' attention spans, use of hands-on experiences with attention to multiple intelligences, promotion of physical movement, high-level thinking, and application of knowledge and skills. Brain-compatible assessment must be of the same nature. Assessment must match the instructional strategies as well as provide the data to drive the future instructional decisions.

Informal Brain-Compatible Assessment

Informal assessment is as simple as watching and listening to students. Day-to-day classroom observations and conversations with students yield a tremendous amount of information about what individuals are understanding, to what level they are applying new concepts, how the class is performing as a whole, what interests are held by the students, and how students work with others in the class. To make these informal observations and conversations valuable for the teacher in driving instruction, he or she must take the time to reflect on what is seen and heard, contemplate what it all means, and take the next steps based on his or her judgments. To make informal assessment valuable for the students, teachers must talk over their observations and resulting insights with their students. Students should be given tips on how to improve without having to worry about scores, grades, or formal judgments. Informal assessment need not always be led by the teacher. Students can learn a great deal from fellow students' observations and comments during discussions.

■ ■ ■

EXAMPLE: INFORMAL ASSESSMENT DURING A MATH CLASS
GRADE 5

Purpose: To quickly assess students' knowledge and understanding of new concepts.

Background: Most teachers have established quick, informal methods of checking students' comprehension to guide instruction during lessons. This may including question-and-answer sessions, roving around the room looking over shoulders at students' work, asking to see thumbs-up or thumbs-down in response to questions asked, and so on. If many of the students in a class seem confused or are completing work inaccurately, the instruction can be immediately altered to teach the concepts in a different manner. If all the students seem to be easily understanding the new concepts, the teacher may move ahead with the topic more quickly than originally planned.

Lesson: Ms. Hartzell, a 5th grade teacher, swiftly assesses her class's level of understanding during mental math problem-solving activities through the students' use of number wheels or whiteboards. While she slowly recites a multiple-step math problem, like $3 \times 8 + 6 \div 5 - 4 = $ ___, her students calculate their answer in their minds. When the teacher finishes the number sentence, the students write down their solutions on their individual whiteboards, or show the correct number on their number wheels. When she gives the word, the student hold their answers up in the air for Ms. Hartzell to see. She can quickly scan the answers to see which individuals may or may not have the correct response as well as get an overall feel for the class's aptitude for the task at hand. After a few rounds of this practice, Ms. Hartzell may determine the whole class needs further practice with this mental math lesson, or she may decide they have mastered that concept and are ready for another challenge. She may also have identified particular students who need individual assistance at a later time. All of this information is gathered through informal assessment during the course of quick exercise.

■ ■ ■

Formal Brain-Compatible Assessment

More formal alternative assessments may include essays, products, performances, short-answer questions, oral presentations, portfolios, exhibitions, and demonstrations. To be considered authentic, or brain compatible, an assessment should involve the students in meaningful, significant tasks that are open-ended, occur over time, and allow for the demonstration of competence in more than one way (Ronis, 2000). This form of assessment involves high-level thinking and usually problem solving, with predetermined high standards that are known by both the teacher and the student. The goal is not to pop-quiz students to discover what they haven't learned but rather to openly identify what is crucial to learn and how it should be demonstrated. In her book *Brain Compatible Assessments* (2000), Diane Ronis details important qualities of brain-compatible, authentic assessments as shown in Figure 7.1. I highly recommend this book for very thorough explanations and examples of practical applications of high-quality assessment.

■ ■ ■

EXAMPLE: FORMAL BRAIN-COMPATIBLE ASSESSMENT GRADE 8, SOCIAL STUDIES RESEARCH PRESENTATION

Purpose: To assess students' knowledge through the use of a rubric, a research project, and a presentation.

Background: A year or so ago, my oldest son, Chad, came home from school griping about an assigned history research project. He felt the teacher was being "stupid" because the assignment was to not only write a research report on a historical figure but also give a presentation about that person. Furthermore, the presentation could not simply be reading the report aloud to the class. As Chad was complaining, I, as a mom and an educator, sat back thinking that the assignment was perfect. Its design required students to understand their chosen historical figure very well. It would not suffice to simply copy or reword information found on an Internet site.

Procedures: Chad had to research information regarding Davy Crockett's life, his contributions to our country, what his time and surroundings were like, and so on. After writing the report and turning it in, Chad also had to prepare his presentation for the

FIGURE 7.1
Characteristics of Brain-Compatible Authentic Assessments

Structure	• Are more public than traditional forms of assessment. • Do not rely on arbitrary or unrealistic time constraints. • Contain questions or tasks that are known beforehand and are not "secret." • Encompass multiple opportunities for demonstration of growth (i.e., portfolios) rather than one-time, stressful experiences. • Include some sort of collaboration with peers. • Allow for a significant degree of student choice.
Intellectual Design Features	• Direct students toward more sophisticated uses of knowledge and skills (i.e., critical-thinking skills). • Integrate tasks and their outcomes. • Assess thinking processes rather than bits and pieces of isolated information. • May involve somewhat ambiguous or "messy" tasks and/or problems to be solved. • Utilize the student's own research or use of knowledge. • Present a challenge that emphasizes depth of knowledge and understanding. • Stimulate and educate so that students can learn from the assessment process.
Grading & Scoring Standards	• Based on clearly articulated criteria and performance standards rather than a curve or norm. • Use performance indicators, which allow students to know ahead of time what excellence looks like (i.e., rubrics). • Make metacognitive activities such as self-assessment and self-reflection part of the total assessment process. • Use a multifaceted scoring system rather than a single numerical grade.
Equity	• Identify hidden strengths rather than weaknesses. • De-emphasize competitive comparisons between students. • Allow for different learning styles, abilities, and interests.

class complete with a semblance of a costume. The presentation was only a few minutes long, but it had a formal rubric of expectations to meet in order to achieve differing levels of success in the overall grade. Chad could use props during the presentation, but not any written notes. This way, the teacher could determine if he had indeed internalized the information read about Davy Crockett. As a follow up to Chad's three-minute talk, a few students in the class were allowed to ask questions about Davy Crockett. As Chad answered these questions, the teacher was able to further assess Chad's knowledge of the research through its application and his own interpretations and conclusions.

The teacher's formal assessment for this project included a written report, a verbal presentation, and the impromptu answering of questions that could prove or disprove application of knowledge. The students were given a rubric in advance for both the report and the presentation, outlining clear expectations for success. Finally, following this multiple-approach assessment process, the students received feedback from the teacher on each component as well as from their peers on the presentations. This is an excellent example of thorough, well-planned, brain-compatible assessment.

■ ■ ■

Teacher as a Coach and the Use of Rubrics

The "old" way of teaching was to teach, and teach, and teach, and then test. This process would determine if the students remembered what the teacher determined to be the most important elements of the instructional unit. As a high school student, I recall having the feeling that some teachers would stand back chuckling when students didn't remember the precise words to fill in the blanks on a quiz; I had the sense that teachers wanted to trick students into failing rather than guide them into succeeding. The "new," or more brain-compatible, way of teaching is more in the role of a coach.

Think about how an athletic coach operates. He or she tells the players the ultimate goal: a touchdown, for example. The coach shows them what that looks like and exactly what plays or strategies are most effective in helping them reach that goal. He or she assists the players, both as a team and individually, with a variety of methods to learn and perform those plays. The coach provides time, resources, incentives, models of the necessary skills, hands-on practice, and even cheerleaders on the side to help each player learn the necessary skills to achieve the goal. If the team does not achieve the touchdown, as hoped for, the coach goes right back to the drawing board to discover new and better ways of achieving success with the players.

Now think about how a teacher can operate as a coach in the classroom. Specify the ultimate goal for the students; don't keep it a secret. Reveal exactly what assessments will be conducted during the course of the unit. Provide them with time, resources, incentives, models, and hands-on practice while you act as their cheerleader as well as their coach. If a student has trouble, provide alternate forms of instruction until he or she understands the concept or skill. Then, if the final assessment reveals the ultimate goal of learning is not yet achieved to the expected standard, go back to the drawing board to discover new and better ways to help students succeed.

Perhaps the best way a teacher can coach for high achievement is through the use of rubrics. A rubric is typically a chart of criteria used by students as an effort and work guide. The same rubric is subsequently used by the teacher as a scoring guide for students' products or performances. It allows the teacher, students, and parents to know up-front what, for example, "excellent" or "good" or "fair" or "poor" looks like and the details of how to achieve at each level.

The best rubrics guide students' work, and the evaluation thereof, through both product criteria and process criteria. Rubrics give the student clear expectations for achieving at varying levels of success (almost a "cheat-sheet" of exactly what to do). We learned in Chapter 2 that setting clear academic expectations for students is one way to alleviate stress. Implementing rubrics is a prime example of doing just that. Prior to starting their work, students should be given samples of work at each level of achievement and be given the rubric that will ultimately score their finished product. Just as a football coach shows videotapes of effective plays and ineffective plays, teachers should show or demonstrate models of each level of achievement defined in the rubric. Empower the student to choose which level of achievement he or she will work toward, leaving no confusion (or possible excuses) for the students! Finally, rubrics give the teacher a fair, specific form of evaluation and feedback for the student and a communication device with the parent as well. It is rather easy for a student or parent to contest a letter grade score when that alone is all that is assigned to a finished product. It is rather easy for a teacher to defend, if ever under scrutiny, an evaluative score when he or she can display, side-by-side, the finished product and the rubric, particularly when the student received the rubric and samples in advance of starting his or her own work. Figure 7.2 shows a rubric used in writing organization in grades 3 through 5.

Feedback

Feedback is a natural, regular occurrence in our everyday lives. Through feedback, we learn cause and effect: Am I wearing the correct shoes for today's weather conditions? No, my feet are cold and wet. Did I say the right thing to my daughter? Yes, she is now grinning with pride. Day in and day out we learn from trial and error as well as from trial and success. Immediate, specific feedback is the most meaningful to us. If I step outside and immediately feel cold, wet feet, I can go back in and change into warmer shoes or boots. I have made the corrections and can almost immediately go on successfully with my day. If I am on an extended vacation and find, only when I am a thousand miles from home, that my feet are cold wearing the shoes I have packed, the feedback and consequence come too late for fast and easy corrections. Instead, I might have to suffer through the trip with cold feet. I might have to spend souvenir money on new shoes. In either scenario, whether prompt or prolonged feedback is received, I can learn from my mistakes.

Feedback in the classroom also occurs naturally, but, in addition to that, it must also occur in a planned, purposeful manner. When prompt feedback is received, the learner can either make a quick correction and move on or proceed with the confidence that he or she is on the right path. One of the most difficult things for a brain to do is to unlearn deeply embedded knowledge or skills (McGeehan, 1999). Just as it is much easier to run back into the house for warmer shoes rather than buy new ones on a trip or suffer with inadequate shoes until the vacation is over, the

FIGURE 7.2

Writing Rubric—Focus on Organization
(3rd–8th Grade Rubric)

Student Name: _____ Date: _____

	ADVANCED (3)	PROFICIENT (2)	BASIC (1)	MINIMAL (0)
Topic Sentence(s) (x4)	Topic sentence grabs reader's attention and summarizes the paragraph content.	Topic sentence states what the paragraph will be about.	Topic sentence is confusing and may not introduce the content of the paragraph.	There is no topic sentence.
Supporting Details (x4)	All sentences are important and relate to the main topic.	There may be a few gaps in information.	Some details support the topic sentence, but others are unrelated.	Details have nothing to do with the topic.
Sequence (x4)	The writing is very easy to follow. Each detail is in order.	There is a beginning, a middle, and an end.	The writing is somewhat confusing. Some sentences should be in a different order.	Sentences are out of order.
Closing Sentences (x4)	Each paragraph ends with a complete summary.	The reader may not be expecting the paragraph to end when it does.	The end of the paragraph is too sudden. It is confusing to read.	There are no closing sentences.

Sentence Structure (x4)	All sentences are complete and flow into the next. Sentences are varied and complex.	All sentences are complete.	Most sentences are complete.	There are many run-on or incomplete sentences.
Spelling (x2)	All words are spelled correctly.	Most words are spelled correctly.	Some words are spelled correctly.	There are many spelling errors.
Grammar (x1)	There is accurate grammar/usage in piece.	There are few grammar/usage errors.	There are some grammar/usage errors.	There are many grammar/usage errors.
Capitalization (x1)	All words are capitalized correctly.	Most words are capitalized correctly.	Some words are capitalized correctly.	There are many capitalization errors.
Punctuation (x1)	All sentences are punctuated correctly.	Most sentences are punctuated correctly.	Some sentences are punctuated correctly.	There are many punctuation errors.
Indents (x1)	There is accurate paragraph indentation.	Most paragraphs are indented.	Some paragraphs are indented.	Paragraphs are not indented.

Scoring = **Total Points** = ___

$$\frac{78}{78} = \underline{\quad\quad} \%$$

125

sooner that academic feedback is received, the easier it is to make the necessary corrections.

In the classroom, it is far easier for a student to learn of his or her mistake, immediately learn how to correct it, practice it more, and reap the rewards of success on the next trial. Without immediate feedback, that student may have continued to practice incorrectly, imbedding incorrect knowledge into the brain. It is demoralizing for a student to learn, after weeks of practicing a skill, that he or she has been doing it incorrectly all that time. Not only does the student need to start over from scratch in relearning the skill, but first the brain has to work hard to unlearn the wrong method. This leads to a situation when simply giving up becomes the easiest option for a student. Some of us probably remember having a college class in which we wrote several papers without any rubric or samples provided ahead of time to clarify the expectations and without receiving any feedback or a grade from the professor until the end of the semester, when it is too late to improve. Very frustrating! Teachers must not do this to their students. The students' brains and egos both need prompt feedback.

So what exactly does feedback look like in a classroom? It is a response that should be taken by the student as a cue for either a change toward improvement or maintenance of the successful status quo, either academically or behaviorally. It may be a letter grade or a narrative comment on the top of a paper. It may be a positive compliment or a lengthy discussion. It may be a scowling expression or a thumbs-up sign. John Hattie (1992) analyzed close to 8,000 studies and concluded that "the most powerful single modification that enhances achievement is feedback. The simplest prescription for improving education must be 'dollops of feedback'" (p. 9).

Feedback may come from the teacher, other adults, classmates, or oneself. Eric Jensen (1998) states that, as a general rule of thumb, students should receive some form of feedback at least once every half-hour during lessons. Jensen (2000) also contends that the most effective feedback is prompt, specific, and multimodal, and comes from differing people including oneself.

Prompt Feedback

As previously discussed, prompt or immediate feedback is most valuable to learners. Letting the student know if he or she is on the right track promotes confidence and more successful learning as the student progresses through the lesson or unit of study.

■ ■ ■

EXAMPLE: PROMPT FEEDBACK
GRADE 8

Purpose: To provide students with prompt feedback regarding their opinions, knowledge, or current progress. Whether this feedback is formal or informal, from the teacher or from peers, it directs next steps for the students.

Informal Sample: In an 8th grade literature class, the students are grouped in literature circles according to student-chosen novels. The student facilitator of one group asks the questions, "Which aunt does Jacob prefer? Why or what evidence from the story supports your answer?" Another student answers, "Jacob likes the plump aunt better, because on page 119 he states . . ." The facilitator asks the other group members whether they agree or disagree with the response. The students, without talking, display either a thumbs-up for agreement, a thumbs-down for disagreement, or a sideways-thumb for partial agreement. Based on this informal feedback from peers, the answering student may ask another student for clarification on his or her disagreement. In this case, the answering student chose a girl showing a sideways-thumb to explain her thinking. She stated that she agreed that the character preferred his plump aunt but had very different evidence from the story. The first student reconsidered his evidence and agreed that the girl's quotes from the text provided a stronger argument for the opinion.

Formal Sample: In the same literature class, the teacher required the students to write responses to particular questions after every third chapter read in the novels. He always returned these assignments the very next day with not only a numerical score indicated, but more important for feedback purposes, narrative comments.

The comments usually consisted of a few positive compliments regarding each student's insights or opinions and always included at least two follow-up questions for the student. These questions were purposefully designed to provoke high-level thinking (drawing conclusions, making inferences, comparing or contrasting, or synthesizing information). The students were held accountable for answering these questions in one of three different ways: They could choose to write and turn in a response to his questions; they could set up a miniconference with the teacher to verbally respond to his questions; or they could discuss his question and their answers with one of their classmates who was reading the same novel. The classmate would then initial on a certain form, for accountability purposes, that the student had indeed completed the required task. In this example, the student was receiving immediate, valuable feedback from the teacher and even from a peer in some cases.

■ ■ ■

Specific Feedback

"Good job!" is very nice to hear but gives the student no definitive information to use in making further learning or work decisions. Feedback must be very specific to assist the learner in knowing exactly what to keep doing and what to change. Using rubrics provides teachers with one vehicle for specific feedback correlating precisely to the work completed. When a rubric is not used, other feedback—whether it be formal or informal, or written or verbal—should be useful and corrective in nature. It should notify the student specifically what is being done correctly and what is being done incorrectly.

A synthesis study of research findings regarding feedback described in *Classroom Instruction That Works* (Marzano, Pickering, & Pollock, 2001) supplies meaningful and practical information for teachers: Following a formal assessment, such as a written test, simply notifying the student whether an answer was right or wrong has a negative effect on achievement. Letting the student know what the correct answer was has a moderate effect on further achievement. The best form of feedback, with the highest effect on further achievement, is providing the student with a full explanation of accurate and inaccurate answers. Furthermore, requiring the students to continue working on the task until they achieve success appears to improve learning and achievement.

■ ■ ■

EXAMPLE: SPECIFIC FEEDBACK
GRADE 5, MATH UNIT TEST DATA

Purpose: To provide students and parents with specific feedback that is useful in steering future learning.

Procedures: Fifth grade teacher Mr. Mulvey wanted to ensure his feedback to students was valuable to them for continued improvement in his math class. Following the first of the three unit tests of the school year, Mr. Mulvey did not simply return the students' tests donned with a percentage or letter grade. Rather, in addition to the overall percentage score, he broke down each student's score according to concepts learned during the unit (see Figure 7.3) and gave that information to each individual as well as to his or her parents. Because Mr. Mulvey's school had a spiral math curriculum, each concept or topic area came up at least one more time in each of the next two units during the school year. With the information provided, each student had an idea of where he or she may need to spend more time and effort in order to reach higher overall achievement in math. A simplistic score on the top of a unit math test would never have driven specific corrections or focus during the next unit of study.

■ ■ ■

Multimodal Feedback

Brain-compatible learning research tells us that students should learn and be assessed using a variety of methods. The good ol' lecture-and-test

---

FIGURE 7.3

Feedback to Students and Parents Regarding Test Scores

Math—Unit One Test Results

Student Name ———————— **SAMPLE** ———— Date ————

Category:	Score:	Class Average:
Overall Score:	72	78
Decimals Only:	56	67
Basic Operations:	90	92
Comparing Decimals:	100	83
Multiplying Decimals:	75	69
Add/Subtract Decimals 1:	50	74
Add/Subtract Decimals 2:	75	55
Decimals & Powers of Ten:	0	59
Story Problems:	50	61

Dear Students and Parents,

Above is a breakdown of the results from the recent Unit One Test. I hope this helps you identify individual areas of strength and weakness, for each student and for the class as a whole. Compare your own results to the class averages.

Note: The overall score is for the entire test. The decimals only score tells what percent you received on ONLY problems involving decimals. The estimation section is left out of this breakdown because it was not a representative sample of that skill.

As you can see, we are, as a class, still weak in some areas, especially multiplying decimals and whole numbers, adding and subtracting decimals, decimals and powers of ten, and story problem solving. We will continue to work on these skills until we master them. Extra time spent at home focusing on them will help progress immensely.

Parents, please review these results with your children, do spend extra time (if possible) focusing on weaker areas, and do contact me with any concerns or questions. Also, please sign and return this form, so that I know you are aware of how your child is progressing in math.

Sincerely,

Mr. Mulvey

Parent Signature: ——————————————— Date: ——————

---

mode does not yield the highest level of knowledge nor the application of the knowledge or skills. Effective teachers are using multimodal strategies such as hands-on discovery, discussion, experimentation, high-level thinking and problem solving, activities involving all multiple intelligences, offering choices, authentic learning and assessment, tying learning to emotions, and collaborative learning for teaching and assessment. Therefore, feedback on all these strategies for instruction and assessment should be just as enriched and complex.

In the "Prompt Feedback" literature class example, you learned about a teacher who provides feedback through scores, written notes, verbal comments, and discussion with peers. Each of these methods is bound to be the most effective for several students in the class, just like different instructional methods are bound to be better for some students than others. Below is a list of multimodal approaches to providing feedback to students. Try to use at least a few of these ideas each day for your students, including additional methods that you may think of as you read this sample list:

- Smile
- Pat on the back
- Letter grade
- Nod of the head
- Verbal compliments
- Percentage score
- Applause
- Discussion
- Written comments
- Verbal suggestions
- Checklist of accomplishments
- Scores/criteria on a rubric
- Token rewards or consequences
- Written suggestions
- Model the skill
- Verbal correction
- Turn the classroom lights off or on
- View a picture or video of the work
- Phone call
- Send an e-mail message
- Ding a bell/buzz a buzzer
- Display a colored flashcard
- Give out or take away play money
- Rank list of scores
- Goal achievement chart
- Whisper in the ear
- Plus or minus symbol
- High-fives
- Written note
- Peer editing
- Thumbs-up or thumbs-down

Feedback from a Variety of Sources

The feedback examples listed above need not only come from teachers. Classmates, students from other classes, any adult in the school, parents, community members, standardized testing companies, student teachers, visitors to the school, and central office staff can provide feedback to students. A student can even provide feedback to himself or herself through reflection and self-assessment. Daniel Druckman and John Swets (1988) wrote of study results in *Enhancing Human Performance: Issues, Theories, and Techniques,* claiming that peer feedback is actually more influential than teacher feedback on long-lasting performance. Because the teacher provides so much feedback, both positive and negative, in the classroom, it is often perceived by students as repetitive and, therefore, insincere. It is thought that the approval or disapproval of peers is a stronger reinforcer for students (Howard, 2000).

■ ■ ■

EXAMPLE: FEEDBACK FROM PEERS
GRADE 3, STORYTELLING PRESENTATIONS

Purpose: To provide the means for students to give each other constructive feedback on their work.

Procedures: Mrs. Rintelman teaches a storytelling unit wherein each student chooses a different book he or she reads many times over, getting to know the story thoroughly. The students are taught the art of storytelling, including the use of props, voice inflection, body movements, and so on. Toward the end of the unit, each student completes a storytelling presentation for the class. If chosen as one of the top three storytellers in the class, that student gives a second presentation for the whole grade level. As each student tells his or her story, Mrs. Rintelman completes a written feedback slip, and every student in the class writes one out as well. Consequently, each student receives feedback from the teacher as well as from about 20 peers. Mrs. Rintelman spends time teaching her students what constitutes valuable, constructive feedback so the students' compliment coupons are not simply written out to say "good job." Rather, the focus is positive, including at least one compliment and one friendly tip for improvement.

■ ■ ■

The Benefits of Authentic Assessment

Assessment and feedback guide learning when designed and implemented correctly. Teachers cannot know what to teach next if they don't know what has been learned. And without receiving feedback, students don't know what they are doing well and what they need to improve. We know that norm-referenced, standardized tests provide us with comparisons of achievement that can help schools draw general conclusions about instructional practices. Typically, standardized assessments treat each student in a uniform manner, are limited in format, and are quite removed from any real-world context. In contrast, authentic, alternative assessments treat students as unique individuals, are far more brain compatible, and are based on classroom instruction.

The education system is moving—albeit slowly—away from the process of using the bell-shaped curve to weed out perceived "weak" students who don't perform well on tests. We are moving into an era in which we know every student is unique and can contribute in our ever-changing world. We exchange the idea that some students must fail for the belief that all students can productively learn. We coach students into attaining the goals by flat-out telling them what they need to know and then working like crazy to help them, through brain-compatible instruction and assessment, until they succeed. In a time when new information is being discovered and learned at an amazing rate, we understand that requiring students to memorize all of it is futile. Far more beneficial for the students and for society as a whole is for them to learn how to be good problem solvers, to be high-level thinkers, and to work collaboratively with others. This desired high level of knowledge and skills will only result from instruction based on a well-planned plethora of authentic assessments and resulting feedback to students that is prompt, specific, and multimodal, and that comes from a variety of people.

133

Implementing Relevant Brain-Compatible Ideas

Assessment

- Keep in mind that tests are just one form of assessment. Use product-based assessments such as models or presentations in addition to or instead of all written tests.
- Also keep in mind that assessment is not the end of learning but should guide continued learning.
- Implement a wide range of assessment practices, both formal and informal.
- Match assessments to the instruction and vice versa.
- Consider students' differing multiple intelligences when designing assessment methods.
- Infuse assessment into daily practices.
- Make assessments as authentic or real-world as possible.
- Try to reserve less than 50 percent of your assessment for proving foundation-level knowledge. Have the larger, more important half be dedicated to the student synthesizing, evaluating, or applying the new knowledge.
- Promote Chapter 2's emotional wellness and safe environment principles in assessment situations.

Feedback

- Remember, effective feedback can be either planned or spontaneous in nature.
- Ensure that feedback to students is prompt and specific, and that it comes from several different sources.
- Allow for logical, natural feedback to occur for students, from the crash of a paper airplane model to the applause from peers.
- Make immediate, interactive feedback part of the learning process so students can avoid learning and practicing something incorrect.

8

Collaboration

THE HUMAN BRAIN IS A SOCIAL BRAIN (SOUSA, 1995). PEOPLE LEARN AND REFLECT through communication and cooperation with others. Most employers put a strong emphasis on hiring people who have the skills to get along well with others and who have experience working collaboratively on teams. While schools do not typically have courses in cooperation or collaboration the way they have math or reading courses, these are important skills that educators should teach and model for their students.

Collaboration, as defined by *The American Heritage Dictionary* (1982) simply means "to work together, especially in a joint intellectual effort." Many important projects, whether being completed in an elementary school classroom or in a business's conference room, depend on collaboration to effectively accomplish the task. Human brains like to create and explore new ideas and then bounce them off someone else. People typically fear the giant risk of implementing a new idea without at least one other person helping with it or at least knowing about it. But because sharing new ideas is risky, effective collaborative groups must have an atmosphere of support and emotional safety (McGeehan, 1999).

The education system is one based on people, so it is naturally a social setting. However, the fact that many people are working together does not necessarily mean that they are working collaboratively and cooperatively. Having a common vision and goals and working collaboratively toward them creates an effective, beneficial climate for a learning community or a school. Teachers and other staff members working successfully in this type of atmosphere are good role models for their students. Just as all adults don't always act cooperatively, children are not born naturally cooperative. In fact, humans are born with quite the opposite disposition—that of being very self-serving in order to have their survival needs met. When hungry, a baby will not turn in a friendly, cooperative manner to share his or her bottle. We would never expect this. However, as children age and mature, we do expect respectful, cooperative attitudes and actions. Therefore, somewhere between infancy and young adulthood, children need to be taught how to cooperate and collaborate.

What is the difference between *collaborate* and *cooperate*? Very little, officially. *The American Heritage Dictionary* defines cooperate as "to work or act together toward a common end or purpose." In terms of classroom practices and instructional strategies, I use "collaborative learning" as a global term describing many types of group work. I use "cooperative learning" to refer to one type of collaboration—the very specific form of instructional grouping practices developed by David and Roger Johnson (1999). Collaborative learning practices, including Johnson and Johnson's cooperative learning model, are brain compatible for the following reasons (Caine & Caine, 1994; Ronis, 2000):

- An innate function of the brain is to search for meaning. Collaborative learning provides the brain with the means to explore new information, typically in a problem-solving situation.
- The brain is social and, therefore, likes to learn from others and with others.
- Working with other people tends to elicit stronger emotional responses to the work. We've learned that emotionally laden information tends to be remembered by the brain easily and permanently. It could be concluded, then, that much of the information learned in a group may be more effectively remembered.
- The brain likes to contemplate varying viewpoints. Multiple viewpoints tend to occur regularly in collaborative learning.
- Working toward a common goal is ingrained in collaborative teamwork. The brain tends to function well with the challenge of a goal, and students like the feeling of success after reaching a goal.
- The brain can understand a large, general concept while simultaneously learning and working with related specific details. Group work is built on this principle and, therefore, is logical to the brain. The task of the group is understood and dealt with as a whole, but the individuals are each contributing different parts.

• Collaborative groups are designed to be supportive and cooperative by nature; competition and the threat it evokes are not present. We know the brain functions best in a nonthreatening setting because it can focus on high-level thinking using its frontal cortex rather than its "reptilian brain" which operates under fight-or-flight conditions.

Collaborative Learning Strategies and Models

In a thriving, successful school, all parties collaborate—teachers, students, administrators, parents, other staff members, school board members, and community members. Entire books are devoted to school climate and collaboration between adults in organizations. For example, in *Building Shared Responsibility for Student Learning* (2001), authors Anne Conzemius and Jan O'Neill describe how collaboration is one of three key components in a framework for a successful school. Student achievement and ongoing improvement are the other two components. For our purposes here, just the topic of student-based collaboration in learning is discussed through the following strategies or models:

• Pair and Share
• Cooperative Learning
• Group Work Within a School
• Collaboration Between School and Community

Pair and Share

It takes only two people to form a group for collaboration. Teachers pair students for a variety of reasons. It may be to work on a project together or to have one student tutor another student, or it may be for purely social reasons like showing a new student around the school. Each of these examples tends to be preplanned or, at least, somewhat formally organized. "Pair and Share" is the name of a partner strategy that is typically less formal and may or may not be preplanned. It is simply the practice of taking anywhere from 20 seconds to 5 minutes to have students turn to a classmate and share a bit of information with each other, discuss their opinions, or ask each other questions.

This collaboration technique is highly brain compatible for three main reasons. First, it allows the two students' social brains to have a minute or so to bounce ideas off each other. Second, it provides emotional safety through trying out an idea or asking a question of just one person rather than openly taking that risk with an entire class. And third, "pair and share" can be the vehicle for providing that 2-minute shift in attention that is necessary after 20 minutes of steady concentration. Examples of successful practice of pairing and sharing include the following:

- **To review prior knowledge.** The teacher partners students to discuss previously learned information and how it relates to the new concept being studied.

- **To correct mistakes.** The teacher partners students to check over each other's work. A partner may suggest improvements or reteach a skill to his or her classmate.

- **To provide lesson closure.** The teacher partners students so they can take turns summarizing the overall objective of the lesson, explaining what they learned, or describing what their favorite parts of the lesson were.

- **To voice an opinion.** The teacher partners students to tell each other about their respective opinions regarding a topic, an answer given in class, or a favorite part of a story's plot.

- **To try out an answer.** The teacher partners students to allow each to tell his or her guess at an answer and receive feedback from one person prior to raising a hand and announcing it to the whole class.

- **To explain a process.** The teacher pairs students to have one person talk through his or her thinking process in how a task was accomplished. Sometimes students learn more easily from a peer than from a teacher's explanations.

Cooperative Learning

Cooperative learning works on the premise that two heads (or more) are better than one. In most careers, people need to work cooperatively in order to develop, make, advertise, and sell a product or service. It is, therefore, beneficial for students to learn to operate under similar circumstances in schools. In Johnson and Johnson's Cooperative Learning model (1999), students in small groups of four to six members work toward a mutual goal. These goals can only be fully attained if and when *all* group members succeed (Ronis, 2000). The atmosphere in these groups is one of teamwork, assistance, and encouragement rather than competition. According to

David and Roger Johnson (1999), two leaders in the field of cooperative learning, there are five basic elements in successful implementation of cooperative learning:

1. Positive Interdependence. The group of students determines a division of labor, information, and resources among the members. Specific roles or jobs are assigned that may include facilitator, timekeeper, recorder, or resource/materials person. Mutual rewards and consequences exist within the group (the whole group will either sink or swim).

2. Face-to-Face Interaction. The students have structured exchanges of giving and receiving ideas, summaries, explanations, and assistance. Everyone contributes and everyone celebrates successes. The idea of synergy is important; the resulting whole is greater than the sum of its parts. The success of the group exceeds what individuals could accomplish on their own.

3. Individual Accountability. One student cannot do all the work while the remainder of the group gets to reap the rewards. Each member must be held accountable for contributing his or her fair share—the teacher must assess not only the achievement of the group but also the achievement of each individual.

4. Interpersonal and Small Group Skills. Students must learn and use the necessary skills for effective teamwork. The skills of communication, leadership, manners, trust, decision making, and conflict resolution must be taught and monitored by the teacher.

5. Group Processing. The teacher must provide the time and necessary skills for the students to reflect on their performance as a whole group and as individual members of a team. Effective processing will provide the group nonthreatening feedback as to how well they function in carrying out their roles, reaching their intended outcomes, and using their interpersonal skills.

Group Work Within a School

Although collaboration between students is easiest to facilitate within one classroom, many schoolwide grouping initiatives and programs are successfully implemented through the planning, effort, and support of staff members. Effective collaboration among the adults is a strong predictor of thriving schoolwide collaboration among students.

Grouping students from different grade levels for a project or program, like grouping within one classroom, is based on collaborative efforts toward a specific purpose or shared goal. In advance of the initiative, teachers should teach the students the necessary communication and group skills required to work cooperatively. This may require particular focus on interpersonal skills between students of different ages; older students may need guidance in understanding the ability levels and social behaviors of younger students, while younger students may need modeling of appropriate behaviors and practice in how to speak assertively to older students. The goals of group work within an entire school may range from tutoring activities to sporting competitions. The following example is a framework for multi-age student groups in a school whose purpose could be academic, social, and/or community service.

■ ■ ■

EXAMPLE: S-TEAMS
K–8 SCHOOL

S-Team stands for Schoolwide Team, with an intentional play on the word *esteem.*

Purpose: To have students work collaboratively in multi-age groups.

Goals: These groups participate in a variety of activities throughout the school year, including reading to each other, tutoring, holiday parties, mentoring, recess friendships, making projects for senior citizens, and raising money or supplies for charities.

Organization: In a kindergarten through 8th grade school, two students from each grade level are assigned to each S-Team. These 16 students are led by a variety of staff member participants including grade-level teachers, special education teachers, specials/allied arts teachers, teachers' aides, etc. The principal has no assigned group but roves among all the S-Teams.

Implementation: S-Teams meet for one to two hours once per month on a Friday afternoon. The schedule and objectives are planned in advance at a staff meeting. When the teams meet for the first time, the team leader facilitates team-building activities, and the group decides on a team name and some goals, within certain guidelines. For example, it is predetermined that the November and December S-Team meetings will have an objective related to community service. Each different S-Team may decide what form of community service to do—one team may decide to collect hats ....d mittens for the Family Sharing Center, another may decide to make Christmas ornaments for area businesses.

■ ■ ■

To successfully implement the S-Team program or something similar to it, the staff must buy into the idea, be willing to plan collaboratively with other staff members, work with a wide range of students, and believe this time away from regular classroom lessons and curriculum is valuable for students. The students are able to benefit from working in relatively small groups, with one adult and with students from each grade level in the school. This builds self-esteem for the younger children, who feel important working with the "big" kids, and also builds the self-esteem of the older students, who can function as mentors for the younger children. When the staff is committed to the program, implementing S-Teams is a fun and rewarding experience for both students and adults.

Collaboration Between School and Community

Whether your school is in a small-town or a large metropolitan area, the community surrounding your school is important to you, and your school is important to that community. Community members, both private citizens and area businesses, want to know the nearby schools are safe and effective learning centers that will graduate bright, productive young adults into society and the workforce. Political and communication issues can arise when the citizens and businesses don't know what actually happens in schools and when school personnel don't recognize important issues out in the community.

An open flow of communication can occur between the school and community through school newsletters, school board meetings, chamber of commerce memberships, and inviting community members into the schools for events or to use the physical building. Something as simple as letting citizens use your school building as a voting site or before and after hours for indoor walking, sporting leagues, scouting troops, or weekend craft fairs can go a long way in establishing positive public relations. Furthermore, once those community members are in the school, even if it is just to walk through the hallways or to use the gymnasium, they'll have a feel for what your school is all about simply from glancing through classroom windows or seeing student work samples in the hallways. The next time you call on one of these citizens' businesses for a donation of some sort for your school, they are likely to be more compliant in helping if they have at least been inside the school. The following is a successful example of a community-related school initiative that occurs at my school in Jackson, Wisconsin.

■ ■ ■

EXAMPLE: COMMUNITY READING EVENT
ELEMENTARY SCHOOL MODEL

Background: The West Bend Joint School District includes not only the 11 schools in West Bend, Wisconsin, but also Jackson Elementary School in the small, neighboring town of Jackson. Jackson is a close-knit community of 5,000 people. Because we are the only public school in Jackson, we are a pretty special entity there; the students in the school are deemed very important in the community. The staff at the school believes it is important for the 480 students to feel connected to and respectful of their community. We have some typical community links like police and fire department safety programs. In addition, our student chorus sings at some area businesses during the holidays, and we send our monthly school newsletter to our business partners. However, none of these practices actually pulled community members into our school to allow them to see our fabulous students and staff hard at work doing what they do day in and day out. Consequently, we began our Community Reading Event.

Purpose: To allow students to meet community members and to allow community members the opportunity to experience being in a classroom reading to students.

Organization: The event is held for about 45 minutes just after the lunch hour one day during American Education Week. An invitation is sent to business leaders, community service workers, school district central office administrators, school board members, and local politicians. At least one community member reads a book in each of the 22 homeroom classes in the school. The school provides age-appropriate books to choose from, or the guest is welcome to bring his or her own favorite children's book to read. He or she may also request a particular grade level or classroom. Following the story, there is typically discussion about the community member's job, what he or she remembers about school, and so on.

Implementation: The community members arrive and gather in one meeting room in the school. They may choose their books, if they haven't brought one along. The principal welcomes them and assigns a teachers' aide to escort the readers to their assigned classrooms. After less than 30 minutes in the classroom, the community members return to the original meeting room for cookies, coffee, and the chance to mingle a bit. They are thanked by the principal for their attendance and each year they all leave smiling, asking to be invited back the next year.

■ ■ ■

To date, Jackson School has hosted two Community Reading Events. Both were quite successful, with a good representation of community members attending, such as the village president, a UPS driver, the local grocery cashier, the school board president, doctors, garden center workers, a firefighter, the chief of police, and the school district's curriculum director. Students love being read to in the first place. But when the story is read by their own dentist or the person who bags their groceries at the store, it is a pretty "cool" experience. The students also get to hear firsthand about their reader's job and have the opportunity to ask questions of him or her.

The community members also love the opportunity to take an extra long lunch break and spend the time with children. Each person who attended the first year wanted to come back the second year. At the end of the event this past November, they again wanted assurance that they would be invited back next year. As an observer in the meeting room with these 25 or more community members, I saw adults who were happy to be briefly working with children as well as having a good time building camaraderie with each other.

Effective Collaboration

Effective collaboration, within a classroom or a whole-school setting, requires more than plunking a few students together at a table. First, students must be taught appropriate social and communication skills for partner or group work. In formal work teams, such as in Johnson and Johnson's cooperative learning model, students must be taught and then practice each of the different team roles they will hold during the work time. These roles may include facilitator, timekeeper, recorder, and resource/materials person. Even in less formal or impromptu groupings, such as in a pair and share model, the students still require prompting and practice in attentive listening and providing meaningful feedback to their partners. Teachers' time and effort allocated to collaboration training for students at the beginning of a school year pays off in efficient, cooperative teamwork throughout the rest of the school year.

In addition to learning *how* to function collaboratively in a group, the students need to know *why* they are working together. Without a clearly defined goal or common purpose for the group, the teacher essentially has a party on his or her hands. A party is a gathering of people who want to have fun socializing—I guarantee students will do this. Collaborative teamwork occurs when the group has a goal to reach and is cooperatively striving to accomplish the tasks at hand in order to achieve success with the goal—students will do this, too, as long as they know the purpose and the expectations for the work.

We know the human brain likes to work collaboratively with other brains. Involving students in group work may take many forms, including the five discussed in this chapter. These types of group work may have very similar or very different purposes, they may involve two students or all students of a school, and they may be formally or informally planned. Regardless of the differences between types of collaborative learning, each model does include two or more students working together to achieve a goal. Synergy is a powerful byproduct of successful collaboration and teamwork—the whole is worth more than the sum of its parts. In other words, the knowledge gained or the product created by students working collaboratively in a group is bound to be of higher quality than if each student worked separately to complete the work.

In each model, students have the opportunity to learn from each other. Each student in a group has unique talents, knowledge, and skills to share. Students enjoy learning from other students. And beyond simply being enjoyable, it is effective for learning because, as the saying goes, to teach is to learn twice. When students can share their own knowledge and skills with others, not only do the "receivers" gain because they learn something new, but the student who is acting as the teacher will solidify his or her knowledge teaching it to others. When I taught 3rd grade, for example, I had to *really* know the rainforest well in order to teach that unit to my students. I knew more about it than anyone else in that classroom. Why should the teacher always get to know every topic of the curriculum the best? I want my students to know more than I know. Maybe teachers should let the students *really* get to know a topic well and then, through collaborative group work, pass that knowledge on to everyone else.

Implementing Relevant Brain-Compatible Ideas

Pair and Share
- Make sure there is a predetermined goal or purpose for the work.
- Partner students frequently, even if just for a two-minute "check-in" on each other's ideas.
- Develop quick ways to determine students' partners, sometimes letting them choose, sometimes with the teacher choosing, and sometimes using random assignment.
- Teach students active listening skills.
- Use pair and share to alleviate student stress in risking an answer in front of the entire class.

Cooperative Learning
- Make sure there is a predetermined goal or purpose for the work.
- Implement particularly for experiments, projects, and group problem-solving situations.
- Train students, in advance, how to function within each role in the group.
- Require that every student carry his or her fair load of the work through individual accountability measures.
- Foster teamwork, not competition.

Group Work Within a School
- Make sure there is a predetermined goal or purpose for the work.
- Remember that staff members' attitudes are the models for students' attitudes.
- Establish ownership and/or buy-in with schoolwide initiatives.
- Involve students in making some appropriate choices within the framework of group initiatives.
- Teach and model collaboration for students.
- Build student self-esteem through multi-age programs.

Collaboration Between School and Community
- Make sure there is a predetermined goal or purpose for the work.
- Involve students in the community and involve community members in the school.
- Give plenty of notice for events/activities and follow up with thank-you cards.
- Show students the importance of the community they live in.
- Show community members what terrific, hardworking students are being developed in your school.
- Plan events that are fun and then smile all the way through them—a smile goes a mile in terms of "P.R."

9

Leadership Strategies to Promote Brain-Compatible Learning

IN EDUCATION, CHANGE DOES NOT HAPPEN OVERNIGHT. ONE TEACHER CAN MAKE a significant difference in the education of his or her students by implementing brain-compatible instructional strategies. However, this teacher must also realize that it will take time to try one or two strategies, assess how they work, make revisions as needed, and try them out again. Once the first couple of strategies have become part of a successful routine, he or she may be ready to try implementing another new idea. It may take years before strategies are implemented from all of the seven brain-compatible fundamentals outlined in this book; this is to be expected. Furthermore, if the hope is to develop a brain-compatible learning environment throughout a whole school, the staff will not only need time, training, and resources, but also effective leadership to guide the change process.

What is leadership? Over time, a wide array of people have defined leadership. Academics, sports fans, politicians, educators, and stockholders all have theories about what constitutes a leader. Bernard Bass (1981) lists the characteristics that differentiate leaders from followers as "a strong drive for responsibility and task completion, vigor and persistence in pursuit of goals . . . originality in problem solving . . . sense of personal identity, willingness to tolerate frustration and delay, the ability to influence other persons' behavior" (McEwan, 1994). Most contemporary researchers, however, have found it more useful to describe what effective leaders actually do rather than what personal traits they have.

Also common to current literature defining leadership is the description of leaders assessing each situation and adjusting their behaviors according to the complexity of the task or goal as well as the composition of the group being led. Many of the general leadership definitions, characteristics, and practices apply in the educational arena. However, educational leadership has some unique principles as well. In order to promote innovation within a school—brain-compatible strategies, for example—the principal, or possibly a different staff member, must be an instructional leader and be aware of stages and reactions involved in the change process.

Instructional Leadership

An instructional leader has the responsibility and privilege to serve as a role model for both the students and staff in a school. For this reason, the leader should live and breathe excitement for learning. The instructional leader should also be a learning expert. This entails keeping abreast of the most recent brain research and all of its implications for learning and teaching. This leader must also be aware of the teaching practices being used in every classroom in the school. Obviously, many of the practices that teachers have used for decades remain very effective today. On the other hand, we now have more thorough insights into the biology of learning through medical advances and the current brain research. The challenge for a leader in a school becomes not only to gain the most up-to-date knowledge regarding learning, but also to ensure that faculty members learn and use that knowledge as well.

A successful instructional leader has the ability to motivate teachers and the intelligence and knowledge required to effectively guide their teaching practices to heighten student learning. "The message from effective instructional leaders is that anyone can be an instructional leader if he or she: has vision; has the knowledge base; is willing to take risks; is willing to put in long hours; is willing to change and grow constantly; thrives on change and ambiguity; and can empower others" (McEwan, 1994, p. 13).

Appropriately, the principal is typically considered to be an instructional leader of a school. However, new instructional innovations certainly do not always stem from the principal. Other staff members can indeed be instructional leaders who initiate change in a school. Be it the principal, or another staff member, or a team of change agents, a leader is always teaching. He, she, or they are the leaders who model their values and goals through decisions, responses, and behaviors; these leaders must walk the talk. In addition to serving as a role model in implementing new initiatives, Smith and Andrews (1989) describe a school's instructional leader as one who

• provides the necessary resources so the academic goals can be achieved;

• possesses the current knowledge and skill in curriculum, assessment, and instructional practices so that the teachers' interactions with the principal lead to improved instruction;

• is a skilled communicator with students, school staff, parents, community members, media, central office personnel, and fellow administrators; and

• acts as a visionary who motivates and facilitates improvement.

In the most effective schools, instructional leadership is a team effort and does not depend solely on the principal. Every school has many committed, competent teachers who need to be tapped as decision makers and guides. The overall goal is for the principal to become the leader of the leaders in a school (Sergiovanni, 1995). Through shared values and leadership, more staff members will take an active role in building quality within the school. This feeling of ownership of improvement and excellence is extremely powerful in achieving successful change.

Change Process

According to Jane Rasp McGeehan (1999), "Leaders of significant change in education enjoy the sweet rewards of success—renewed teachers and staff, students eager to learn, and supportive community members." Great educational leaders set high standards for all people involved in the school while continuously striving for improvement. More often than not, making meaningful improvements in a school involves significant change. Leading people through a change process is both difficult and rewarding. If change is fostered incorrectly by a leader, it can be an adversarial, exhausting battle. If facilitated correctly, change can be a collaborative, exhilarating, and gratifying journey.

Hard work and lots of time will always be part of an effective change process. If change seems too easy, it probably isn't a true, enduring change.

Some of the literature on school change assumes that adoption is the same as implementation. Adoption of an innovation is easy. It's the implementation that takes the time and effort. And even successful implementation of a change in a school setting is not enough. In order for lasting improvement to occur, the implementation must be sustained over a long period of time to become part of the ordinary life in the school community (Sergiovanni, 1995). Several recommendations have been provided from a variety of researchers, businesspeople, and educators on how to be successful initiating and facilitating a significant systemic change.

First, within the school setting, the principal cannot institute a change alone. It is far more effective to consider the principal as the leader of the change-facilitating team. A second level of change facilitators is usually identified as the researchers. These people typically are lead teachers, department chairpersons, and resource teachers. And a third level of facilitators is typically a group of teachers who could be called pioneers. These people serve the change process primarily by modeling the use of the new practices, disseminating information to others, and providing support to the other pioneers (Sergiovanni, 1995). An effective leader of change values taking risks, recognizes grassroots movements toward improvement, and promotes teamwork with shared decision making.

A school will progress through several phases during any major change. The leader needs to help teachers face the fact that institutionalizing a major change will take approximately five years, with ups and downs along the way. During these years, the staff will move through eight predictable phases of the change process (see Figure 9.1). In order to effectively facilitate change, it's necessary for the leader to not only personally be aware of the eight phases of change and work within them, but also to teach the staff what is entailed in the change process (Myrah & Erlauer, 1999a).

While progressing through the stages of change, staff should realize that these phases, although linear, may contain chaotic times. This chaos is okay. For it is through some of the most disorganized, upsetting circumstances that the most creative solutions and ideas are discovered. Sadly, what occurs all too frequently in organizations is that people give up too early. As seen in Figure 9.1, as change is initiated, interest and effort are sparked. Shortly after that, however, people will naturally become skeptical; rewards and success are not reaped immediately, so

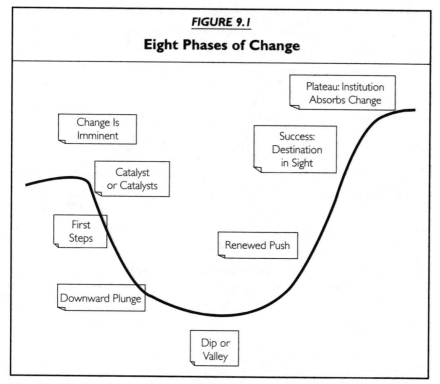

FIGURE 9.1

Eight Phases of Change

Plateau: Institution Absorbs Change

Change Is Imminent

Success: Destination in Sight

Catalyst or Catalysts

First Steps

Renewed Push

Downward Plunge

Dip or Valley

Adapted from *Tools for Change Workshops,* by R. Champion, 1993, Oxford, OH: National Staff Development Council.

frustration sets in. At this same time, external chaos is usually occurring as well; people are threatened by change, so some will refuse to participate and will resent that resources are being poured into a new initiative without proof of long-lasting results. It can be very easy to abandon the initiative when the organization reaches that dip or valley stage. This is a crucial time for the educational leader or leaders to step up the support by distributing more monetary resources, time, training, and commendations for effort to rekindle the commitment in the new practices. Just on the other side of that dip stage is the upward momentum toward achievement, success, and true adoption of the initiative.

Finally, merely understanding change theory will not result in a true, productive change in a school system. A firm, detailed vision statement is also necessary. Only when the school's policies, procedures, structure, and practices totally support the organization's vision will strategic alignment be in place (Schwahn & Spady, 1998; Senge, 1994). As a result of working with hundreds of school districts, Schwahn and Spady (1998) have identified five reasons why change initiatives fail and five corresponding change rules to facilitate productive change (see Figure 9.2).

Five-Year Plan to Steer a School Toward Brain-Compatible Learning

Steering a school in the direction of brain-compatible instruction is not a quick trip but rather a long journey. It will require careful planning and

---

FIGURE 9.2
Change Reasons and Rules

Five Reasons Change Did Not Work	Five Rules for Successful Change
1. Your purpose wasn't compelling enough—the staff didn't own it and couldn't state it in their own words from memory.	1. People need a compelling reason to change.
2. You didn't develop it correctly—all the stakeholders were not involved.	2. People need to have ownership in the change.
3. You didn't start using it immediately—the values, mission, and beliefs didn't become part of all decisions and actions.	3. People need to see that their leaders are serious about change.
4. You didn't align the people—some personnel treated the strategic plan as optional rather than the way we all proceed.	4. People need to have a concrete picture of what the change will look like for them personally.
5. You didn't align your organization—the system didn't change according to the new vision but remained status quo.	5. People need organizational support for the change.

Adapted from "Why Change Doesn't Happen and How to Make Sure It Does," by C. Schwahn and W. Spady, 1998, *Educational Leadership, 55*(7), p. 45–47.

execution. Within a five-year change process toward brain-compatible learning, the principal can expect to see particular tendencies each year. The principal, and the other instructional leaders, must manage those tendencies openly and supportively. While each school's path will be different, most leaders can expect to move through the journey in this general fashion (McGeehan, 1999; Myrah & Erlauer, 1999b).

Year One

The school has a reason to change and embarks on the journey. Training begins and leaders emerge. Along with some superficial implementation, some saboteurs also arise. The principal should take time to build trust and develop a shared vision. Change theory should be part of the training for staff so they understand the phases they will go through individually and as a school. Leaders should be providing resources, offering support for taking risks, and promoting respect and teamwork while the school is in the first stages of trial implementation.

Year Two

Teachers beyond just the instructional leaders and "pioneers" ask for more information and training on brain-compatible teaching strategies. Rather than sending more individuals off to brain-based learning seminars, at this point it may be most cost efficient to bring an expert to your school. Bringing an expert to your school also guarantees that all staff members are privy to the same information. When a critical mass of teachers moves forward learning about brain-based practices, this creates great energy within the school. Other district personnel, parents, and/or community members realize something new is occurring. This "outside" interest has the potential to be controversial and confrontational. Toward the end of this second year, the change dip or loss of focus is typical. The change leaders must continue to be cheerleaders for the cause. Communication with other district personnel and parents should be frequent and forthright to inform and even to elicit help. However, the principal and other instructional leaders must also accept controversy as a part of change. Restating the vision and nurturing pride in the hard work helps move the staff out of that dip or valley stage when the temptation is high to simply revert to old ways.

Year Three

A feeling of commitment is renewed. A strong need for more resources and time to further implement practices becomes apparent. Shared leadership becomes the norm as teachers look to each other for additional ideas. The principal should take advantage of this upbeat time to marshal district support for increased time and additional resources to continue the drive forward toward total implementation of brain-compatible learning. Now that the vast majority of teachers are using brain-based learning strategies in their classrooms, begin collecting data for comparison purposes of improved student achievement and performance. Encourage visitors to spend time in the school observing the positive changes; this helps the staff to feel pride and celebration.

Year Four

Staff members feel like experts in teaching with brain-compatible strategies and want to assess the practices occurring in classrooms. They need to begin assessing student achievement data. Some staff will be ready to delve even deeper into the ever-expanding brain research and may form small study groups. The principal needs to provide for that higher level of training. These teachers may become the resident experts and trainers of trainers for new staff joining the school. In year four it becomes important to thoroughly implement assessment and reflection processes and to share the resulting information with all the stakeholders. Although improved student achievement is seen, a few holdouts on the staff make cynical or negative comments. These folks may never change. This is okay as long as the leaders do not let the negative few spoil the enthusiasm and progress of all the others. It may be time to counsel a negative teacher into making the choice to either come on board or jump ship to a different building.

Year Five

The brain-compatible instructional strategies are institutionalized; they are simply the way things are done now. Through studying the results of assessment, reflecting and upgrading of practices will occur for continued improvement. Networking with other schools and making formal presentations to share knowledge and ideas are recommended. The time has come when the principal and other leaders are doing less instructional leadership and more service, support, and facilitation to keep the good things going. This leadership team will want to document the practices and related student achievement to share with others, including the school board and community members. These instructional leaders may even be ready to discover a new initiative to complement the successful practices in place.

Team Leadership

Involving others in the change process, working through the systemic phases and individual concerns, and aligning the goals, people, and structures while holding the guiding vision as the goal is the way to facilitate long-lasting improvement in a school. The change process is not always led solely by the school principal. In fact, the most effective changes are typically led by a team of leaders. This team should be enthused, confident, and knowledgeable about the new practices, in this case brain-compatible learning. As instructional leaders, the team members should be visionary, hard working, and resourceful. They should also be risk-takers and effective communicators. It is important for these leaders to understand the stages of change a school will progress through and be able to help others work through each of those stages. They themselves must persevere through the obstacles and difficult times along the journey while, at the same time, serving as role models and cheerleaders for the rest of the staff. Over the years, these instructional leaders will be valued and trusted if they offer the staff the necessary support and resources. And, as leaders, it would be helpful for them to keep in mind as improvement occurs that to give credit is much more powerful in the long run than to take all the credit.

Brain-Compatible Instruction in Context

Students today deserve an outstanding education based on current brain research. This is not meant to suggest that everything teachers and schools have done in the past is wrong, but rather that we have new information, based on the actual biology of the brain's learning, that can improve education. Reaching the point of having consistent brain-compatible instruction within a school certainly involves more than a one-shot teacher inservice training on strategies. It involves progressing through a long change process led by knowledgeable, visionary, motivating instructional leaders. A thorough understanding of the change process and exemplary instructional leadership skills will dramatically strengthen the likelihood of the brain-compatible practices being implemented correctly and permanently.

Brain-compatible instructional strategies work because they are based on research, match common sense, and involve teaching the way students learn. Brain-compatible learning is not a trendy educational fad like all those that have come and gone over the years. Rather, brain-based learning should free educators from those waxing and waning trends; if a new teaching practice or strategy does not match how the brain learns, it should be dismissed. When many of us were trained to be teachers, we heard and read about how to teach but not much about how students truly learn. Fortunately, many of those teaching strategies we learned in college are effective with students. Today, after a couple of decades of medical advances and, consequently, remarkable discoveries about the brain, teachers can learn why all those tried-and-true methods have worked with our students. Even more exciting is the fact that we can discover many new brain-compatible instructional strategies that will help our students learn more successfully than ever before.

Bibliography

Abbott, J. E. (2001). Emotional intelligence, part 2: The social brain and conversations in school. *Today's School—Shared Leadership in Education, (2)*3, 34–39.

American heritage dictionary (2nd college ed.). (1982). Boston: Houghton Mifflin Company.

Armstrong, T. (1994). *Multiple intelligences in the classroom.* Alexandria, VA: ASCD.

Barth, R. S. (1980). *Run school run.* Cambridge, MA: Harvard University Press.

Bass, B. (1981). *Stogdill's handbook of leadership: A survey of theory and research.* New York: Free Press.

Begley, S. (1996, February). Your child's brain. *Newsweek,* 55–62.

Bell, A. (2001, Spring). FERPA—The keys to compliance. *A Legal Memorandum.* Reston, VA: National Association of Secondary School Principals.

Bloom, B. S. (1976). *Human characteristics and school learning.* New York: McGraw-Hill.

Bolman, L. G., & Deal, T. E. (1984). *Modern approaches to understanding and managing organizations.* San Francisco: Jossey-Bass.

Bonstingl, J. J. (1996). On the road to quality: Turning stumbling blocks into stepping stones. *The School Administrator, 53*(7), 16–21.

Brooks, J. G., & Brooks, M. G. (1999). The courage to be constructivist. *Educational Leadership, 57*(3), 18–24.

Brynie, F. H. (1998). *101 questions your brain has asked about itself but couldn't answer until now.* Brookfield, CT: Milbrook Press.

Caine, R., & Caine, G. (1994). *Making connections: Teaching and the human brain.* Menlo Park, CA: Addison-Wesley.

Conzemius, A., & O'Neill, J. (2001). *Building shared responsibility for student learning.* Alexandria, VA: ASCD.

Cooperative Learning Center. (2000). *The Cooperative Learning Center at the University of Minnesota* [Online]. Available: http://www.clcrc.com/item.html#essays.

Druckman, D., & Swets, J. (1988). *Enhancing human performance: Issues, theories, and techniques.* Washington, DC: National Academy Press.

Education and the Supreme Court: The 2001–2002 Term. (2002, July 10). *Education Week, 21*(42).

Erlauer, L., & Myrah, G. (2000). Bringing brain-based learning to your school district. *Wisconsin School News, 55*(1), 4–13.

Fogarty, R. (1998). Intelligence-friendly classrooms: It just makes sense. *Phi Delta Kappan, 79*(9), 655.

Fullan, M. (1993). *Change forces: Probing the depths of educational reform.* Bristol, PA: The Falmer Press, Taylor & Francis, Inc.

Gardner, H. (1983). *Frames of mind: The theory of multiple intelligences.* New York: Basic Books, Inc.

Ginott, H. (1975). *Between teacher and child.* New York: Avon.

Glasser, W. (1998). *The quality school: Managing students without coercion.* New York: Harper Collins.

Goleman, D. (1995). *Emotional intelligence: Why it can matter more than IQ.* New York: Bantam Books.

Hattie, J. A. (1992). Measuring the effects of schooling. *Australian Journal of Education, 36*(1), 5–13.

Hord, S. M., Rutherford, W. L., Huling-Austin, L., & Hall, G. E. (1987). *Taking charge of change.* Alexandria, VA: ASCD.

Howard, P. J. (2000). *The owner's manual for the brain.* Austin, TX: Bard Press.

Jensen, E. (1996). *Cerebral showcase* [Motion picture]. Del Mar, CA: Turning Point Publishing.

Jensen, E. (1997). *Brain-compatible teaching that "skyrockets" learning!* A Staff Development Resources presentation, Torrence, CA.

Jensen, E. (1998). *Teaching with the brain in mind.* Alexandria, VA: ASCD.

Jensen, E. (2000). *Different brains, different learners—how to reach the hard to reach.* San Diego, CA: The Brain Store, Inc.

Johnson, D. W., & Johnson, R. T. (1999). *Learning together and alone: Cooperative, competitive, and individualistic learning.* Boston: Allyn & Bacon.

Johnson, D. W., Johnson, R. T., & Holubec, E. (1998). *Cooperation in the classroom.* Edina, MN: Interaction Book Company.

Joyce, B., & Showers, B. (1988). *Student achievement through staff development.* New York: Longman.

Krynock, K., & Roob, L. (1999). Problem solved: How to coach cognition. *Educational Leadership, 57*(3), 29–32.

Kumar, D. D. (1991). A meta-analysis of the relationship between science instruction and student engagement. *Education Review, 43*(1), 49–66.

Lupien, S. (1998). Cortisol levels during human aging predict hippocampal atrophy and memory deficits. *Nature Neuroscience, 1*(1), 69–73.

Marzano, R. J., Pickering, D. J., & Pollock, J. E. (2001). *Classroom instruction that works: Research-based strategies for increasing student achievement.* Alexandria, VA: ASCD.

McEwan, E. K. (1994). *7 steps to effective instructional leadership.* New York: Scholastic, Inc.

McGeehan, J. R. (Ed.). (1999). *Transformations: Leadership for brain-compatible learning.* Kent, WA: Books for Educators, Inc.

Myrah, G. E. (1996, February). *The evolution of change: Must it hurt.* Paper presented at the 30th Annual Special Education Conference, University of Wisconsin-Oshkosh, Oshkosh, WI.

Myrah, G. E., & Erlauer, L. (1999a, March). *How to steer your school to brain-based learning.* Paper presented at the ASCD National Conference, San Francisco.

Myrah, G. E., & Erlauer, L. (1999b). The benefits of brain research: One district's story. *The High School Magazine, 7*(1), 34–40.

Okogbaa, G., & Shell, R. (1986, December). The measurement of knowledge worker fatigue. *IIE Transactions, 18*(4).

Patterson, J. L. (1993). *Leadership for tomorrow's schools.* Alexandria, VA: ASCD.

Ronis, D. (2000). *Brain-compatible assessment.* Arlington Heights, IL: SkyLight Training and Publishing, Inc.

Ross, J. A. (1988). Controlling Variables: A meta-analysis of training studies. *Review of Educational Research, 58*(4), 405–437.

Schwahn, C., & Spady, W. (1998, April). Why change doesn't happen and how to make sure it does. *Educational Leadership, 55*(7), 45–47.

Senge, P. (1994). *The fifth discipline fieldbook: Strategies and tools for building a learning organization.* New York: Doubleday Press.

Sergiovanni, T. J. (1992). *Moral leadership: Getting to the heart of school improvement.* San Francisco: Jossey-Bass.

Sergiovanni, T. J. (1995). *The principalship: A reflective perspective.* Boston: Allyn & Bacon.

Shaw, G. (2000). *Keeping Mozart in mind.* San Diego, CA: Academic Press.

Shore, R. (1997). *Rethinking the brain.* New York: Families and Work Institute.

Smith, W. F., & Andrews, R. L. (1989). *Instructional leadership.* Alexandria, VA: ASCD.

Sousa, D. (1995). *How the brain learns.* Reston, VA: National Association of Secondary School Principals.

Sousa, D. (1998). *How the brain learns: More new insights for educators.* A presentation on August 18, 1998, in Port Washington, Wisconsin.

Sprenger, M. (1999). *Learning and memory: The brain in action.* Alexandria, VA: ASCD.

Stiggins, R. J. (1994). *Student-centered classroom assessment.* New York: Macmillan College Publishing Company.

Sylwester, R. (1995). *A celebration of neurons: An educator's guide to the human brain.* Alexandria, VA: ASCD.

Tomlinson, C. A., & Kalbfleisch, M. L. (1998). Teach me, teach my brain—a call for differentiated classrooms. *Educational Leadership, 56*(3), 52–55.

Wisconsin Council on Children and Families. (1999). Critical windows of development. *Brain watch—Great beginnings: The first years last forever.* Author, *1*(2), 1–2.

Wolfe, P. (2001). *Brain matters: Translating research into classroom practice.* Alexandria, VA: ASCD.

Index

choices, student
  for assessment, 67–70
  in decision making, 70–73
  in learning, 63–67
  for motivation, 73–74
  for research projects, 59–62
  value of, 59
Chugani, Harry, 86–87
chunking information, 55
circadian rhythms, 89, 90
classroom
  behavioral expectations for students
    within, 31–34
  behavior in, improving, 15–16
  collaboration within, 137–139
  decision-making in, 71
  decorating, 109–110
  environment of, teachers and, 20–38
  movement in, 47–49
  posting scores in, and stress, 18–19
  sense of community in, 21–23
  smell of, 110–111
Classroom Instruction that Works (Marzano,
  Pickering, Pollock), 82, 128
classroom management plan, 32, 33*f*
classroom rules, 31–34
clock-sheet, 23
coaches
  vs. teachers, 28–29
  teachers as, 121–123
collaboration, 135–146
  within classroom, 137–139
  vs. cooperation, 136
  definition of, 135
  effective, 144–145
  importance of, 135
  within school, 139–141
  between school and community,
    141–144
  strategies of, 137–144
color, and memory, 110
community
  collaboration between school and,
    141–144
  sense of, 21–28
    within classroom, 21–23
    within school, 23–28
community reading event, 142–143
community service project, 24–25
complex questions, problem solving with,
  102
concept, new. *See* new concepts, learning

Concern-Based Adoption Model, 3, 3*f*
consequences for breaking classroom rules,
  32
content
  demonstrating immediate and future
    use of, 54–58
  relevant, 53–58
Conzemius, Anne, 137
cooperation, 138–139
  vs. collaboration, 136
  definition of, 136
cooperative group assignment, 66–67
cortex, 9–11, 12–13, 59, 85
cortisol, 17, 103
counting, movement and, 47–48
cross-grade-level relationships, 25–26
current events, problem solving with,
  100–101

decision making, involving students in, 70–73
decorating classrooms, 109–110
dehydration, 43
dendrites, 11, 13, 42, 97
desert research project, 59–60
differentiating assessment, 68–69
directions, wording, 54
discovery learning, 54, 57, 98
downtime for learning
  within day, 89–91, 111
  within lesson, 91–95
drawing responses, 70
Druckman, Daniel, 132

elves, answers from (project), 25–26
emotional arousal, 13
emotional intelligence, 13–16
Emotional Intelligence (Goleman), 13
emotional quotient (EQ), 13–14
emotional safety, 19–38, 138
emotional wellness, 21
endorphins, 103
*Enhancing Human Performance: Issues,
  Theories, and Techniques* (Druckman and
  Swets), 132
enrichment for brain, 97–112
  through music, 103–109
  through physical environment, 109–111
  through problem solving, 97–102
environment
  emotional, creating safe, 19–38
  physical, enrichment for brain through,
    109–111

presentations
 formal assessment through, 119–121
 research projects, 61–62
 storytelling, 132–133
principal
 as change facilitator, 150
 as instructional leader, 148–149
problem solving
 with complex questions, 102
 with current events, 100–101
 enrichment for brain through, 97–102
 with gamelike activity, 101
 with global issues, 98–100
project-based learning, 59–62
prompt feedback, 126–128
protein, 41–42

questions, complex, problem solving with, 102
quiz, improving achievement on, 50

rainforest destruction, brainstorming on, 99–100
rapport
 between classmates, 22–23
 between teachers and students, 37–38
RAS. *See* reticular activating system
Rauscher, Frances, 108
reading comprehension, 68–69
reading event, community, 142–143
re-explanation, 84–85
referral slip, 16
reflection
 importance of, 82
 20-2-20 rule for, 84–85
relationship management, 14
relationship skills, developing, 14–15
relaxing effect of music, 103, 104–105
relevant content, 53–58
repetitive rhythms, 103
reptilian brain, 7–9, 137
research projects
 formal assessment through, 119–121
 student choice for, 59–62
reticular activating system (RAS), 7–9
reviewing, 57–58, 84–85
Rocky (film), theme from, 28, 105
Ronis, Diane, 119
rubric, 29–31, 121–123, 124f–125f
rules, classroom, establishing, 31–34

safe environment, creating, 19–38
Salovey, Peter, 14

Santa, letters to (project), 25–26
school
 behavioral expectations for students within, 34–36
 collaboration between community and, 141–144
 collaboration within, 139–141
 decision-making in, 71–73
 five-year plan for brain-compatible, 152–155
 sense of community within, 23–28
scores, posting, and stress, 18–19
second language, 88–89
self-awareness, 14, 15–16
self-esteem, 21, 64
self-management, 14, 15–16, 32
self-motivation, 14
senior citizens, children helping, 25
sense of community. *See* community, sense of sense of smell, 8–9
September 11, 2001, brainstorming on, 100–101
serotonin, 42
short-term memory, 13, 45, 81
sleep, 45
smell
 of classroom, 110–111
 sense of, 8–9
snacks, 41
social studies research presentation, 119–121
song(s)
 alphabet, 103, 109
 for celebration, 28
 for inspiration, 105
 for memory, 107–108
 for relaxation, 104–105
spatial intelligence, 63, 65f
specific feedback, 128–129, 130f
spinal cord, 7
standardized tests, 114–116
standing, 48–49
S-Teams, 140–141
Stiggins, Richard, 114
storytelling presentations, 132–133
stress, 16–19
 caused by posting scores, 18–19
 dehydration and, 43
 fear and, 17
 physiological effects of, 16, 17f
 teachers decreasing, 17, 20f
 teachers increasing, 18–19, 20f
stretching, 48

About the Author

Laura Erlauer is an elementary school principal. Her professional background includes teaching kindergarten, 3rd grade, and 7th grade, and serving as a coordinator for gifted and talented students. She has provided consultation and workshops for school districts and has been a speaker at local and national conventions on the topic of brain-compatible learning. Erlauer has authored and coauthored journal articles on the topic as well.

Erlauer received her bachelor's degree in Elementary Education with a minor in Early Childhood Education from Concordia University in Mequon, Wisconsin, and her master's of science degree with a principal license and a curriculum license from Cardinal Stritch University in Milwaukee, Wisconsin. She can be reached at Jackson Elementary School, W204 N16850 Jackson Drive, Jackson, WI 53037. Phone: 262-335-5475. Fax: 262-677-1594. E-mail: lerlauer@hotmail.com.

Related ASCD Resources: The Brain and Learning

At the time of publication, the following ASCD resources were available; for the most up-to-date information about ASCD resources, go to http://www.ascd.org. ASCD stock numbers are noted in parentheses.

Audiotapes
Brains and Education: A Partnership for Life by Marian Diamond (#299231)
The Brain and Leadership by Bonnie Benesh (#299301)
Building Brain-Based Schools by Barry Raebeck (#299089)

Multimedia
The Human Brain Professional Inquiry Kit by Bonnie Benesh (#999003)

Networks
Visit the ASCD Web site (http://www.ascd.org) and search for "networks" for information about professional educators who have formed groups around various topics, including "Brain-Based Compatible Learning." Look in the "Network Directory" for current facilitators' addresses and phone numbers.

Online Courses
Go to ASCD's home page (http://www.ascd.org) and click on "professional development" to find the following courses and tutorials.
ASCD Professional Development Online Courses: *The Brain* and *Memory and Learning Strategies*
ASCD Online Tutorials: *The Brain and Learning*

Print Products
Educational Leadership, November 1998, "How the Brain Learns" (#198261)
Brain-Based Learning Electronic Topic Pack (#197194E)
Brain Matters: Translating Research into Classroom Practice by Patricia Wolfe (#101004)
Education on the Edge of Possibility by Geoffrey Caine and Renate Nummela Caine (#197021)
Teaching with the Brain in Mind by Eric Jensen (#198019)

Videotapes
The Brain and Learning Series (#498062)
The Brain and Mathematics (2 videos) (#400237)
The Brain and Reading Series (3 videos) (#499207)

For more information, visit us on the World Wide Web (http://www.ascd.org), send an e-mail message to member@ascd.org, call the ASCD Service Center (1-800-933-ASCD or 703-578-9600, then press 2), send a fax to 703-575-5400, or write to Information Services, ASCD, 1703 N. Beauregard St., Alexandria, VA 22311-1714, USA.